# MAN—HERE and HEREAFTER

# MAN—HERE and HEREAFTER

*Whence came we and whither do we go?*

*By* M. L. ANDREASEN

"When I consider Thy heavens, the work of Thy fingers, the moon and the stars, which Thou hast ordained; what is man, that Thou art mindful of him? and the son of man, that Thou visitest him? For Thou hast made him a little lower than the angels, and hast crowned him with glory and honor. Thou madest him to have dominion over the works of Thy hands; Thou hast put all things under his feet.... O Lord our Lord, how excellent is Thy name in all the earth!" Psalm 8:3-9.

**TEACH Services, Inc.**
PUBLISHING
www.TEACHServices.com • (800) 367-1844

**Facsimile Reproduction**

Copyright © 2005 TEACH Services, Inc.
ISBN-13: 978-1-57258-310-8 (Paperback)
Library of Congress Control Number: 2004115761

**TEACH Services, Inc.**
PUBLISHING
www.TEACHServices.com • (800) 367-1844

# Chapters

# CHAPTER ONE

# Man Here and Hereafter

AMONG the many interesting subjects pertaining to this world that men study none is of greater importance and value—apart from the question of Deity—than the study of man. Whence we came and whither we are going have always been fascinating problems, and have occupied the mind of man from time immemorial. It would seem as if the last word on this subject should have been said long ago; but, in spite of much discussion and philosophic speculation, men are not agreed on the fundamental facts, nor, indeed, on the definition of the terms used in the discussion.

It is clear, of course, that no agreement can be arrived at until these vital factors are settled. In any debate it is indispensable to understanding and progress that all terms be clearly defined. In this discussion it is of utmost importance that we understand such terms as "soul," "spirit," "life," "death," "mortal," "immortal," "eternal," "everlasting," "destruction," "heaven," "hell," "grave," and others. In due course these terms will come in for discussion and definition. It is also important that we agree on certain rules of procedure. We would suggest the elimination of all conjecture and hearsay evidence, and hold strictly to the accepted forms of proof. It need hardly be added that the Bible will be considered final authority, no distinction being made between the Old and the New Testament.

What, then, is man? This question was asked by the psalmist ages ago, and by him partially answered. "When I consider Thy heavens, the work of Thy fingers, the moon and the stars, which Thou hast ordained; what is man, that Thou art mindful of him? and the son of man, that Thou visitest him? For Thou hast made him a little lower than the angels, and hast crowned him with glory and honor. Thou madest him to have dominion over the works of Thy hands; Thou hast put all things under his feet: all sheep and oxen, yea, and the beast of the field; the fowl of the air, and the fish of the sea, and whatsoever passeth through the paths of the seas. O Lord our Lord, how excellent is Thy name in all the earth!" Psalm 8 :3-9.

From these verses we note that man was "made" by God, "Thou hast made him;" that he was but little inferior to the angels, "a little lower than the angels;" that he was king of creation, "crowned;" that he was given a kingdom, "dominion;" and that he was superior, and ruled the lower creation, "put all things under his feet: all sheep and oxen," etc. We learn also from verse 4 that God is "mindful of him" and visits him.

All these statements are important. They put man on a very high plane. He is God-made; he is king; he is ruler of the brute creation; he is but little below the angels. He is worthy of God's notice; he is capable of association with God. Yet they do not fully answer the question, "What is man?" For that we must go to the original record of creation as found in the book of Genesis.

The first book of the Bible presents a history of the beginning of things: "In the beginning God created." Genesis 1 :1. In the primeval darkness God appeared, and said: "Let there be light: and there was light." Verse 3. Day by day creation proceeded until the sixth day, when "God said, Let Us make man in Our image, after Our likeness." Verse 26. "So God created man in His own image, in the image of God created He him; male and female created He them." Verse 27.

In the second chapter of Genesis the creation of man is mentioned a little more in detail. There the record reads that "the Lord God formed man of the dust of the ground, and breathed into his nostrils the breath of life; and man became a living soul." Verse 7.

These two accounts comprise all the record we have of the

creation of man as recorded in Genesis, and to them we shall now give our attention.

We note that man was "created;" that he was created by "God;" that he was created "in the image of God," "in His own image," "in Our image," "after Our likeness;" that man was "formed" "of the dust of the ground;" that God "breathed into his nostrils the breath of life;" and that "man became a living soul."

As this discussion does not concern itself with the question of evolution, we need not dwell long on the word "created," but only note it in passing. Three times in verse twenty-seven of this first chapter is this word used to denote God's work in making man.

God formed man of the dust of the ground. To form is to make or construct out of existing material; to shape or fashion with hand or tools; to give shape; to mold; to put into a particular or specified form. From this definition it would appear that in forming man God took dust of the ground as His material, and out of it fashioned into the particular or specified form that He had in mind the being called man. Every organ and part of man was complete and ready to function; but as yet there was no life. God then breathed into man's nostrils "the breath of life; and man became a living soul."

According to this account, two acts of God constituted the creation of man: first, the forming of man from the dust of the ground; and, second, the breathing of life into his nostrils, making him a living soul. Man, therefore, is composed of dust of the ground into which is breathed "the breath of life."

Our next inquiry should concern itself with a study of the two elements that made man "a living soul." Of these two there will be no difficulty concerning the first. Man is made of dust. His body consists of the elements of earth, the exact proportions of which are known. According to the best authorities, the chemical content of man's body is as follows:

| Constituent | Per cent in human body |
|---|---|
| Oxygen | 66.0 |
| Carbon | 17.5 |
| Hydrogen | 10.2 |
| Nitrogen | 2.4 |
| Calcium | 1.6 |
| Phosphorus | .9 |
| Potassium | .4 |
| Sodium | .3 |
| Chlorine | .3 |
| Sulphur | .2 |
| Magnesium | .105 |
| Iron | .005 |
| Iodine | Trace |
| Florine | Trace |
| Other elements | Traces |

All these elements are contained in the earth. It is, therefore, strictly and literally true that man is formed of the dust of the ground. From the dust he came, and to dust he will return when the final dissolution of the body takes place.

In regard to bodily function and structure, man has no special superiority over the beasts. It is true that in some functions—as in the use of the hands—man is vastly superior to animals. But it is also true that some animals have certain senses much more developed than has man. The sense of sight is developed to a very high degree in eagles, that of smell in certain strains of dogs and other animals. So, also, is hearing very acute in some beasts; others live much longer than man. While we incline to the belief that even physically man, generally speaking, is superior to animals, the advantage is not always apparent.

After man was formed from the dust of the ground, God "breathed into his nostrils the breath of life; and man became a living soul." In these words is recorded the act that made man alive. Before "the breath of life" was imparted by God Himself, the lifeless body lay prone on the earth, unable to function, without personality, lifeless. Then came the life-giving "breath" from God, and man became an individual, a personality, a living soul. The union of the breath of life with lifeless clay made man a living soul, a responsible personality, capable of understanding and appreciating God, of thinking, of willing, of loving. A new thing had come into existence, a being in the image of God, capable of reproducing himself,—one that could not merely see as did the animals, but perceive; not merely be conscious, but self-conscious; one that could look at the stars of heaven, and also peer into the secret recesses of his own heart.

As this marvelous change from inert clay to active, pulsating, self-conscious life was the result of God's breathing into man's nostrils "the breath of life," we immediately inquire if this "breath of life" was different from that given to animals. On this matter the Scriptures do not leave us in doubt. The same word used of man in Genesis 2:7 is used of animals in Genesis 7:15, where they are said to go "in unto Noah into the ark, two and two of all flesh, wherein is *the breath of life.*" That it is the same "breath of life" that was breathed into Adam's nostrils is further emphasized in verses 21 and 22, where the beasts of the earth are said to die, both fowl and cattle and beasts and creeping things, "all in *whose nostrils* was *the breath of life.*" Since the words in the texts are the same in all cases, we cannot escape the conclusion that "the breath of life" given to man is the same as that given to animals; that it is life from God, the principle of life; that as God is the Author of life and as He is one being, so His life is one life; and that there is no life but such as God gives.

The question may now arise as to what effect "the breath of life" in the nostrils had on the animals. In the case of man, we learned that he became "a living soul." What did the animals become? On this subject also the Scriptures are very plain. Even as man became a living soul, so did the animals. The Hebrew words for "living soul" are *nephesh chaiyah,* and are used four times in the first chapter of Genesis to describe the lower forms of animals. Verses 20, 21, 24, 30. See margin of verses 20 and 30. These words also occur in Genesis 2:19, where Adam gives names to "every living creature" (Hebrew: "every living soul"). Also in Genesis 9: 10, 12, 15, 16 and in Leviticus 11:46 the animals are called "living souls." In each of these instances the English translation is "living creatures," but the original is the same as the word used of man in Genesis 2:7.

Our study thus far has led us to the conclusion that man is God-created; that he is made of the dust of the ground, even as are the animals; that the breath of life was breathed into his nostrils; that he became a living soul; that God likewise gave to all animals the breath of life; and that they also are called living souls.

It would be a hasty conclusion, however, to think that because man and animals are created by the same God, because all have been given the breath of life by Him, and because all are called living souls, therefore there is no difference between man and beast. *There is a world-wide difference. Man was created in the image of God; the beasts were not.* In the next chapter it will be clearly pointed out wherein man differs from the brute creation.

The texts quoted in this chapter give the story of man's creation. They tell what we know of man's nature as revealed by God Himself. So far we have read nothing of an "immortal soul." We have read of "a living soul;" but that term is applied to man and beast alike. We have read nothing of an "immortal spirit;" but we have read of "the breath of life" bestowed without partiality upon both man and beast. Yet there is a difference—a great gulf—between man and the lower creation. Just what is that difference?

# CHAPTER TWO

# *Do All Men Have Immortality?*

Is MAN immortal? Does any part of him survive death and live on forever? If so, what part survives, and under what conditions?

It should be noted that the question does not concern itself with the future immortal life that is the heritage of all the faithful. Nothing could be clearer than the promise of everlasting life to the believer. John 3:16. The time will come when those who seek immortality shall obtain eternal life, which is brought to light through the gospel (Romans 2:7; 2 Timothy 1:10); hence we need not discuss the question of everlasting life for those who, cleansed and redeemed, are Christ's.

The question is, rather, if God created man immortal; if at creation some undying principle was incorporated into man's being that made him incapable of death; if, whether man appreciates and values life or not, he *must* live on, if not in glory then in eternal misery. On the answer to these questions hangs the problem of eternal torment with all its consequences. If man cannot die, then everlasting suffering is possible. If he can die and does die, suffering will sometime be at an end.

It might be well at this juncture to inquire into the meaning of the words "soul" and "spirit." Do they signify the same thing, or is there a distinction between them?

The Hebrew word for soul is *nephesh,* and occurs 745 times in the Old Testament. Four hundred seventy-three times it is translated "soul;" 118 times "life" or "lives;" 29 times "person;" 15 times "mind;" 15 times "heart;" 11 times "body" or "dead body;" 4 times "will;" twice each "appetite," "lust," "thing." Five times (Leviticus 19:28; 21:1; 22:4; Numbers 5:2; 6:11) it is rendered "the dead." In all, the word is translated 43 different ways, all from the same original word *nephesh,* "soul."

The Greek word for soul is *psuche,* and is used 105 times in the New Testament. It is translated "soul" 58 times; "life" 40 times; "mind" 3 times; "heart" twice; "us" and "you" each once; in all, six different ways.

The Hebrew word for spirit is *ruach,* and occurs in the Old Testament 442 times. It is translated by 16 different English words, such as "spirit" 232 times; "mind" 97 times; "breath" 28 times; also "anger," "smell," "blast," "courage," "air." Its equivalent in Greek is *pneuma,* which will be found in the New Testament 385 times. This is translated by four different English words: "life," "spirit," "ghost," and "wind." The Hebrew of the Old Testament has one more word from which "spirit" is translated, *n'shahmah.* This word occurs 24 times, and is translated five different ways: "inspiration," "breath," "blast," "spirit," and "soul."

From the preceding it will be seen that the words "soul" and "spirit" are derived from three Hebrew and two Greek words, and that they are translated in more than sixty different ways. We would draw from this the conclusion that the translators of the Bible believed these words to be comprehensive ones, not capable of being rendered into one or two English equivalents. And such, indeed, is the case. The context and the sense of the passage must largely guide in the selection of the correct English word.

It will also be noted that anyone who wishes to confirm his own opinion can here find Biblical support for it by a partial or narrow interpretation. If, for instance, one should insist that the soul really means the "heart," he could find 15 places in the Old Testament where it is so translated. Should another insist that "mind" is the correct meaning, he also could find 15 places as proof.

And so with "spirit." One might insist that the spirit is only "wind," and cite 97 scriptures as proof; another might claim "ghost" as the proper meaning, and produce 92 texts to prove it. Under these circumstances, what are we to believe?

It is clear that no narrow or partial view will suffice as an explanation. No one of the sixty or more different words gives the whole meaning. All the passages wherein the words occur must be examined, and their meaning weighed. Only thus may a correct understanding be arrived at. But this is a tremendous task. It involves the critical examination of seventeen hundred passages as well as their context. It is much easier to take only a few of these—such as would sustain our own idea—and ignore the rest. But the conclusion arrived at would be no truer than those of the blind men who had been detailed to examine and report upon the size and shape of an elephant. Being led up to the beast, one grasped the tail, and accordingly made his report that an elephant was like a rope. Another took hold of the leg, and reported that an elephant was like a log. One had found the ear, and to him the elephant was flat and limp as a pancake; while the one who examined the tusks reported the elephant to be hard and smooth and made of bone. Each of these reports was true in itself, but none gave a true view. It is methods such as these that cause divergent Biblical opinions.

It is obviously impossible in these chapters to reproduce and examine each of these texts at length. Besides, this has been done by others. All we need to do here is to give the results. And this we shall proceed to do.

"Spirit" is the breath of life, which in the beginning was breathed into Adam's nostrils, causing him to become a living soul. It is the principle of life from God, imparted to man and beast alike. Genesis 2:7; 7:15, 21, 22. It is "the universal principle imparting life from the Creator." It is to man what steam is to an engine. It is as the current of electricity causing the motor to operate. It is impersonal, powerful, God-given.

"Soul," on the other hand, is not impersonal, but individual. It might be said to be the principle of life as embodied in an individual. While it is used of any animate being, whether human or animal, it denotes individual life as differentiated from the mere principle of life.

It is interesting to note that of the 851 times "spirit" is used in the Bible, though translated in more than forty different ways, 762 times the translation accords with the above definition of the impersonal, universal principle of life, while of the 850 times that "soul" is used, 770 are in harmony with the definition of individual personal existence.

In these definitions we are in harmony with most Biblical authorities. Thus Jacobus in "A Standard Bible Dictionary" says: "The word 'soul' stands for the principle of life as embodied in individuals, while spirit is the same principle as cause underlying the constituted life."

Hastings' "One Volume Dictionary of the Bible" says: "Soul is used in the Old Testament for any animated being, whether human or animal," while "spirit is the universal principle imparting life from the Creator."

"The International Standard Bible Encyclopedia" says, under "soul": "The 'spirit' (*pneuma*) is the outbreathing of God into the creature, the life principle derived from God. The 'soul' (*psuche*) is man's individual possession, that which distinguishes one man from another and from inanimate nature."

Accepting these definitions as true and Biblical, we believe "spirit" to be the impersonal principle of life, given to Adam in the beginning, and which at death returns to God who gave it. Ecclesiastes 12:7. As this is the "principle of life," "universal life," "impersonal," and as this same life was given to all created beings, man and beast alike (Genesis 7:21, 22), we are not here concerned with the question whether this life is immortal or not, as immortality cannot be conceived of as apart from personality; and any successful attempt to prove the spirit immortal would thereby prove beasts also to be immortal. The breath of life came from God. It goes back to God. It is the impersonal, universal principle of life, the breath of life. In the same sense that it came from God it goes back to Him. It need only be said in passing that of the more than eight hundred times "spirit" is mentioned in the Bible as applied to man or beast, not once is it spoken of as immortal, or deathless, or never-dying, or anything of like import. This, of course, is only what we would expect, and the Bible does not fail us.

We have now reduced the proposition to a consideration of the soul. The body is not immortal; the spirit is not immortal. Is the soul? What does the Bible say of the immortal soul?

To many who have been accustomed to hear "the immortal soul" spoken of familiarly, it must come as a shock to know that nowhere in the Bible is the soul spoken of as being "immortal," "eternal," "undying," or "deathless." Though referred to 850 times, not once is immortality predicted of it. This indeed is remarkable. It can hardly be considered as a mere happening. If the Bible is supposed to teach the true doctrine, and if we are possessed of an immortal soul, this tremendous fact should not only be mentioned once, but scores and hundreds of times. It should be reiterated again and again, and the truth of it pressed home. What shall we say, then, when there are 850 chances to do so, and not once is it done? Either the Bible is criminally negligent in this important matter or else the belief in inherent immortality is not Bible doctrine.

We would, first of all, therefore, impress upon the reader the significance of the fact that with abundant opportunity to stress the doctrine of the immortality of the soul, the Bible fails even to mention it. While this is negative proof, it is, nevertheless, very interesting and important.

But we would not build a doctrine on a negative proposi-

2

tion; hence we now inquire if the Bible anywhere commits itself to any doctrine as to the nature of the soul. To illustrate: If the Bible nowhere speaks of the soul as being immortal, does it, on the other hand, say that the soul is capable of dying, and that it does die? If it says this, the case is complete. Stronger proof could not be asked.

The Bible says this very thing: "The soul that sinneth, *it shall die.*" Ezekiel 18:4, 20. This, of course, would be impossible if the soul were immortal. But, as has already been shown, the Bible does not say that the soul is immortal, but just the opposite. Hence the Bible is consistent with itself.

It must not be supposed that the texts we have quoted are all that deal with this phase of the subject. The reader may at his convenience look up the subject in any good Bible concordance, and find abundant evidence of the position here taken. Or he may, without any concordance, consult such texts as Revelation 16:3; Psalm 33:19; Isaiah 10:18; Acts 3:23; James 5:20. "Dead body" in the following texts is "dead soul" in the Hebrew: Numbers 6:6; 19:13; Leviticus 21:11; Haggai 2:13. The Hebrew in Numbers 23:10 is: "Let my soul die the death of the righteous." The same is true of Judges 16:30. Job 36:14 in the original reads: "Their soul dieth in youth."

If the statement that God "only hath immortality" (1 Timothy 6:16) is true; if man is "mortal" (Job 4:17); if "this mortal must put on immortality" (1 Corinthians 15:53); if "the gift of God is eternal life" (Romans 6:23); if only "he that hath the Son hath life" (1 John 5:12); if God guarded the way to the tree of life lest men should "eat, and live forever" (Genesis 3:22); it would seem clear that man does not by nature have immortality, but that if he is to obtain it he must "seek for glory and honor and immortality" (Romans 2:7).

Lest any be confused by these statements, let us hasten to add that the Bible clearly teaches eternal life as the reward of the righteous. "God so loved the world, that He gave His only-begotten Son, that whosoever believeth in Him should not perish, but have everlasting life." John 3:16. The only point we are making is this: The Bible does not speak of an immortal soul; hence man does not have inherent immortality. Eternal life is a gift (Romans 6:23) given to His own (John 10:27, 28), which only those have who have the Son (1 John 5:11-13).

Let us lay hold on Jesus Christ through whom immortality is made possible to all sinners who put their trust in Him.

# CHAPTER THREE

# Man Made "in the Image of God"

MAN was created in the image of God. Genesis 1:27. We do not read of any other creature so created. It would, therefore, be well to inquire into the meaning of this expression. This would also cause to stand out in bold relief the difference between man and the lower creation.

We believe that man was created in the image of God with reference to three distinct aspects—the physical, the intellectual, the spiritual. We shall proceed with the proof.

Of Adam it is said that he "begat a son in his own likeness, after his image." Genesis 5:3. These are substantially the same words used in Genesis 1:26, 27, where God's statement is: "Let Us make man in Our image, after Our likeness." We understand that when a son bears the likeness of his father, is in his image, he has some physical resemblance to his parent. This would not exclude other characteristics, but the first thought would certainly be that of physical likeness. While we would not enter into a discussion of the Father as a spiritual being, whom no man has seen or can see, we would call attention to the fact that when a description is given of Him He is spoken of in the terms of a man, with hands, feet, face, etc. Exodus 33:21-23; 24:9-11.

We know that to some this may seem grossly materialistic, and we are not insisting on an acceptance of this view. We know that God is a spirit, or rather, as the Revised Version reads in the margin, "God is spirit." John 4:24. We would not try to define this further. All we insist on is that where God is spoken of so as to make Him comprehensible to our faculties, He is mentioned as possessing bodily characteristics akin to those of man. Further than this it is not necessary for us to go.

Whatever physical likeness man may have to the great

God above—as mirrored and evidenced in the incarnation of the Son—is not, however, the most important phase of man's being made in the image of God. As the intellectual is of more importance than the mere physical, so man's likeness to God in his intellectual capacity is of transcending importance.

We believe that man is created in the image of God with respect to his intellectual nature. "Put on the new man, which is renewed in knowledge after the image of Him that created him." Colossians 3 :10. Note the wording: "Renewed in knowledge after the image of Him." Hence to be created in the image of God, includes the intellectual image as well as the physical.

Man is the only creature that walks upright. He was intended not to be confined to this earth, but to have the upward look. God endowed him with powers of observation and reasoning, of reflection and will. Of all earth creatures, he alone is capable of understanding God, he only can fathom His plans. In this he is not only superior to the animals, but he is so far removed from them that the gulf is impassable.

A dog may look at a book and see all that a man sees, but the dog is debarred from ever having the least comprehension as to the meaning of what he sees. He may watch his master put wood on the fire, but he never would think of keeping a fire going to keep from freezing to death.

A monkey may be taught to look at the Pleiades, but their meaning must forever remain a closed book to him. Such ideas as time, space, abstract ideas, self-determination, are beyond the reach of the highest of created beings below man. John Burroughs rightly says in "Ways of Nature": "Animal life parallels human life at many points, but it is on another plane. Something guides the lower animals, but it is not thought; something restrains them, but it is not judgment; they are provident without prudence; they are active without industry; they are skillful without practice; they are wise without knowledge; they are rational without reason; they are deceptive without guile."

Animals have many remarkable traits, and some of their senses are very highly developed indeed, but no amount of training or instruction could ever convey to them the faintest idea of heaven or hell, of the fourth dimension, or of the fact that all right angles are equal. Though animals may approach very close to thinking, we have no actual proof that they do so. They have brains and can be taught many things, but the power of reason, at least of abstract reasoning, is apparently denied them.

Many times has the experiment been tried of hanging a bunch of bananas in a monkey cage so high that it could not be reached, and then placing a number of boxes in the cage, which, if they were piled one on top of another, would enable the monkeys to get the food. Scores of monkeys were in the cage, but it occurred to no one of them to take the boxes and make a platform sufficiently high to get at the food, and that in spite of the fact that they were starved, and that hence all their attention must have been riveted on the suspended bananas. This experiment—as well as many others of like nature—has been tried so often and with like results that men have despaired of ever finding any case where it is indisputable that reason is used by an animal. We all know of cases where unusual intelligence has been exhibited and animal instincts prevailed, but the world has yet to find a single case of pure reason.

Man is an intellectual being, capable of measuring the depths of the heavens as well as of exploring his own soul. He is not only conscious, but self-conscious. He can examine himself and sound the purity of his motives. He bridges the chasms and tunnels the mountains. He chains the lightnings and utilizes the mighty forces of nature. He builds machines that, like a bird, fly through the air, and, like a fish, descend to the deep. He parts asunder continents and harnesses the mighty waterfalls. He speaks, and his voice is heard around the world; he commands, and the earth gives forth its treasure. He weighs the suns in a scale and marshals electrons to do his bidding. He discovers the timetable of the stars and delves into the secrets of nature's laboratory. Truly, he is but little below the angels, yet only a child of the dust— created in the image of God, but formed of clay.

We believe that man was created in the image of God with respect to his spiritual nature. "Put on the new man, which after God is created in righteousness and true holiness." Ephesians 4:24. Man is created in righteousness and true holiness "after God;" that is, even as God has these attributes, so man has been created with them.

Man is a moral being, capable of understanding right and wrong. In this capacity he stands definitely differentiated from the lower creation. No dog ever carried back the meat it had stolen from the butcher. Beauty, virtue, holiness, are terms foreign to brutes. Man alone has capacity for God. He is a partaker of the divine nature. 2 Peter 1:4.

The divine nature includes all that God is, His character. Man was created, not with a neutral disposition, but with definite tendencies toward the right. "God hath made man upright." Ecclesiastes 7:29. We need not believe that his character was perfected,—for character is developed, not created,—but we must believe that his predisposition was toward right conduct. He was not created undecided, nor was his character fixed. His was rather a state of childlike innocence, with character as yet untried by test.

The determining factors in character development are discipline and will. The first of these is not pertinent to our discussion here, so it will be passed over. The second—will —should have some consideration.

"Will" may be defined as the power to choose or determine a course of conduct and to direct the energies in carrying out its determination. This choice is God-given. Joshua 24:15.

It carries with it responsibility for the consequences of the choice. Psalm 62:12. As the will thus determines destiny, it becomes of supreme importance in any discussion of man's nature and destiny. "God has given us the power of choice; it is ours to exercise. We cannot change our hearts, we cannot control our thoughts, our impulses, our affections. We cannot make ourselves pure, fit for God's service. But we can *choose* to serve God." The will, says one writer, "is the governing power in the nature of man,—the power of decision, of choice. Everything depends on the right action of the will." "This will, that forms so important a factor in the character of man, was at the fall given into the control of Satan."

Shortly after Adam was created, God told him: "Of every tree of the garden thou mayest freely eat: but of the tree of the knowledge of good and evil, thou shalt not eat of it." Genesis 2:16. The prohibition was clearly stated, and Adam understood it. The penalty for transgression, "Thou shalt surely die," was also stated. Verse 17. In spite of this, Eve "took of the fruit thereof, and did eat, and gave also unto her husband with her; and he did eat." Genesis 3:6. God could have stopped them from eating as He later hindered their access to the tree of life. Verse 24. But He chose not to do so. God did not interfere with their power of choice, even though He knew the consequences—to them and to Himself. To Adam and Eve it meant death; to God it meant the giving of His Son. Yet God gave His Son rather than interfere with man's free will—an indication of God's valuation of it. From this we may learn to treasure the will as one of God's choicest blessings to man.

Man is chiefly will. His life consists in making decisions, which are acts of will. Speaking, walking, eating, loving, hating, may all be done separate and apart from each other, but none of them—or any other conscious function—can be done apart from will. Will is a constituent part of all of them. It is interwoven in every conscious act; it is a vital part of every soul activity.

From the sacred regard in which God holds the will, as evidenced by the incalculable price that He paid rather than interfere with Adam's freedom, we draw the conclusion that in the will we have the choicest blessing of God to man in creation. Man is a free moral agent. God created him so. That freedom may be misused, as in the case of Adam, but in the right use of the will lies the future and eternal happiness of man. Without freedom of will man becomes an automaton—less than a man, a brother to the ox. With freedom of will and a right exercise thereof man becomes a candidate for heaven, for immortality, for glory.

If we were to answer the question concerning the difference between man and beast, we would say that the difference lies not so much in bodily structure as in the intellectual and spiritual realms. In those two spheres the difference is not merely one of degree, but of kind. They constitute in a special sense "the image of God," in which man was created. They place man immeasurably above the brute creation, and make salvation and eternal life possible for those who seek them.

Man, therefore, is created in the image of God with reference to the three aspects of the physical, the intellectual, and the spiritual. To a great degree the image has been lost; but, though partially effaced, it has not been entirely obliterated. The restoration of the image of God in the soul is the aim and object of the plan of salvation. Man, fully restored, shall again reflect the glory of his Maker. Christ "shall see of the travail of His soul, and shall be satisfied." Isaiah 53:11.

It may be that at this juncture some will remark that a very important factor has been omitted in the discussion of man's creation. Is not God immortal? And if man is created in God's image, is not man also immortal? To this the answer may be given that God is indeed immortal, but that this does not necessarily make man so, even though he bears the image of the divine. God has many attributes other than immortality. He is omnipresent, He is omnipotent, He is infallible. That, however, does not make man so. Man is not all that God is. So the fact that God has a certain attribute does not make man the possessor of it. To draw any such conclusion would be beyond reason.

This question, however, should not be thus summarily dismissed; it is a most important one, and should receive careful consideration. Momentous are the issues that hang upon the answer. If man has immortality by creation, if he cannot die though his body be laid to rest, but must live on somewhere, what is his condition after he departs this life? Are the majority doomed to endless torture in hell, where death ever evades them though they pray for it? Shall the joy of the redeemed forever be neutralized by the fearful knowledge that somewhere in God's universe flesh of their own flesh and bone of their own bones are in endless torture? Did God in creation make man so that He Himself can never end man's existence, not even after man is thrown into hell? Or *can* God end man's sufferings but does not choose to do so? If man is immortal, every being that ever lived is *now* somewhere and alive! Stupendous and fearful is such a thought! Where are they? And in what condition? Can they return to earth and communicate with friends by means of séances?

The thought of endless torture is so terrible that some would rather believe that after a shorter or longer period in purgatory most persons will be saved. Others think that there will be a second period of probation; while still others believe that there will be a final judgment after which the wicked will be destroyed and the righteous saved. If we had our choice, and know that all could not be saved, we would certainly wish the last to be true. After every effort had been made to save the lost, and they would not be saved, we could only wish that they might be "as though they had not been." However, it is not our wish but God's word that counts. God does all things well. So we rest the results with Him. The question now before us is this: Is man immortal? To that we shall now address ourselves.

# CHAPTER FOUR

# The Hellish Doctrine of Hell

W E HAVE thus far established from an examination of the Scriptures that, though "spirit" and "soul" are mentioned in the Bible more than sixteen hundred times with reference to man and beast, not once is it said of either of them that they are immortal or eternal or undying or anything similar. We have dwelt upon this fact as an important one, for it would seem that if man were possessed of an immortal soul or spirit, that fact should be made much of, and sixteen hundred opportunities to stress this should not be let slip by. But for some reason—and we conceive it to be a good one—not once is the soul or spirit said to be immortal.

On the other hand, we have found that the Bible very definitely states that the soul is capable of dying. We now come to an important question: If man is not immortal by nature, if he does not have an immortal soul or spirit, is there anything that survives death? "If a man die, shall he live again?" Or is death the end of all existence?

To this—as to all vital questions—the Bible gives a definite answer. Man is made with longings for eternity, with capacity for knowing God, and is told to seek for "immortality." Romans 2:7. "This mortal must put on immortality." 1 Corinthians 15:53. "The gift of God is eternal life." Romans 6:23. Statements such as these could be multiplied greatly. Indeed, the very gist of the gospel is that men "should not perish, but have everlasting life." John 3:16.

We may, therefore, state with all confidence that while "no murderer hath eternal life abiding in him," "he that hath the Son hath life" and they "that believe on the name of the Son of God . . . have eternal life." On the contrary, "he that hath not the Son of God hath not life." 1 John 3:15; 5:12, 13.

We cannot emphasize too strongly that the point at issue is not the question of eternal life. We believe in eternal life, and we believe it because the Bible teaches it and because all true Christians may say, We ourselves "have passed from death unto life." 1 John 3:14. The question at issue is rather this: Does man possess by nature, by creation, or by transmission, an immortal soul, incapable of dying, and must this soul live on regardless of man's destiny? This proposition we unhesitatingly reject as un-Biblical, as unworthy of God, and as a reflection on God's character.

We have already shown that belief in inherent immortality, in an immortal soul, finds no support in the Bible. The reader is referred to the preceding chapters for proof of this. On Biblical grounds we therefore reject the popular belief in the mythical immortal soul. We also reject this belief as inconsistent with a true view of God and as tending to place Him in a false light. This chapter, and the following ones, will deal with this phase of the subject.

We have noted before that belief in an immortal soul compels us to believe that every soul that has ever lived on the earth is now alive *somewhere*. This is patent and clear. If the soul is immortal and cannot die, it must be alive and be somewhere. But this is an awful thought. Millions and millions of souls who have departed this life are still living, and are somewhere. Where are they, and in what condition?

The old theology taught that the blessed souls, upon the dissolution of the body, winged their way to heaven and joined the celestial throng in their never-ending praise to God, while the damned souls departed to Hades, there to suffer the torments of the lost. The first of these propositions will later engage our attention. We shall now deal with the second one.

It is evident from the Bible that not all will be saved. Many will be lost. These lost ones, according to popular theology, are now in hell, suffering tortures of all kinds. They will be there not only until the judgment day, but as long as the saved will enjoy their celestial bliss—ever throughout eternity. There is no cessation to their agony, no respite in their suffering. Day and night they are in torment—wishing for death; but death flees from them. And, according to the theory, this hell is now in existence. Souls are now in torment. Millions are now in excruciating pain, cursing God and one another.

True, judgment has not as yet been pronounced upon them, and there might be some question as to the justice of throwing them into hell before their cases have been heard and passed upon; but the theory of the immortal soul requires such treatment. They are not permitted to die and await the judgment. In fact, they cannot die. Nor are they permitted to enter heaven. Hence they must go to hell.

This doctrine of a never-ending hell has caused many to question the justice of God. It would seem only right that everyone should be punished according to his deserts; but to put a man to unending torture for a smaller or a greater offense would hardly seem just. Men here on earth gauge the punishment to the nature of the crime. There is a certain standard of justice that men try to follow. Some offenses deserve and receive capital punishment. Others are given lighter sentences. While ideal justice is impossible to man, some approximation to it is aimed at.

Some crimes appear so heinous to man that mob violence is sometimes resorted to. A poor, half-demented wretch commits some revolting crime. He is apprehended by the mob, a confession is wrung from him, he is perhaps tortured awhile, then a noose is placed around his neck, his body is riddled with bullets, and he is at last burned at the stake. We shudder at such a scene. We turn with loathing from the details of the execution. We wonder how men can have part in such violence. We feel that whatever the crime, the law should have been permitted to take its course.

But to whatever depths men will go in their desire to mete out punishment, we feel sure that there are some things even a mob would not do. Wrought up to a frenzy by a recital of the crime, they might tear the wretch to pieces, they might torture him, they might gash him with knives, they might burn him with irons, and gouge out his eyes; but after a while they would be satisfied. If the wretch were still alive, and someone should conceive the idea of trying to restore him for the purpose of inflicting more torture, we might even believe that there are men who would do that. But we cannot believe that anyone would indefinitely continue such a program. If one were in possession of miraculous powers to keep the criminal alive in spite of the tortures, men would after a while sicken of the sight, and cry, "Enough! let the wretch die." We should indeed despair of humanity were we to believe otherwise.

The doctrine of eternal punishing in hell-fire compels men to believe that God will do the very thing that human beings, even under the greatest provocation, would refuse to do. Being cast into the lake of fire, men would naturally die, cease to exist. However, if the doctrine of inherent immortality were true, God has so ordered it that they cannot die. He has given them immortal souls. They must suffer forever. They are kept alive for the purpose of torture. Little children, old men, and maidens, according to this false teaching, all are made to live by the power of God that they may be unendurably tormented. Day and night throughout eternity their screams resound through the vaults of hell. They curse God, they writhe in agony; but God does not see fit to end their torment. They must suffer on forever. Such is the belief of those who teach the hellish doctrine of hell.

Lest the reader think we have overdrawn the picture, let me quote from a little work called "The Light of Hell," by Rev. J. Furniss. This book is being printed and circulated today, the copy from which these quotations are taken bearing on the title page the inscription: "Tracts for Spiritual Reading." It was published by P. J. Kenedy, New York, 1880, and has the approbation of William Meacher, vicar-general.

"In hell there are not two or three hundred prisoners only. Millions on millions are shut up there. They are tormented with the most frightful pains. These dreadful pains make them furious. Their fury gives them strength, such as we never saw."—*Page 5.*

"Listen to the tremendous, the horrible, uproar of millions and millions and millions of tormented creatures mad with the fury of hell. Oh, the screams of fear, the groanings of horror, the yells of rage, the cries of pain, the shouts of agony, the shrieks of despair of millions on millions! There you hear them roaring like lions, hissing like serpents, howling like dogs, and wailing like dragons. There you hear the gnashing of teeth, and the fearful blasphemies of the devils. Above all, you hear the roaring of the thunders of God's anger, which shakes hell to its foundations. But there is another sound!

"There is in hell a sound like that of many waters. It is as if all the rivers and oceans of the world were pouring themselves with a great splash down on the floor of hell. Is it, then, really the sound of waters? It is. Are the rivers and oceans of the earth pouring themselves into hell? No. What is it, then? It is the sound of oceans of tears running from the countless millions of eyes. They cry night and day. They cry forever and ever. They cry because the sulphurous smoke torments their eyes. They cry because they are in darkness. They cry because they have lost the beautiful heaven. They cry because the sharp fire burns them.

"Little child, it is better to cry one tear of repentance now than to cry millions of tears in hell. But what is that dreadful, sickening smell?

"There are some diseases so bad, such as cancers and

ulcers, that people cannot bear to breathe the air in the house where they are. There is something worse. It is the smell of death coming from a dead body lying in the grave. The dead body of Lazarus had been in the grave only four days. Yet Martha, his sister, could not bear that it should be taken out again. But what is the smell of death in hell? St. Bonaventure says that if one single body were taken out of hell and laid on the earth, in that same moment every living creature on the earth would sicken and die. Such is the smell of death from one body in hell. What, then, will be the smell of death from countless millions and millions of bodies laid in hell like sheep?"—*Pages 8, 9.*

And this, according to the diabolical theory, shall go on as long as God Himself exists. Note these attempts to measure the length: "Think of a great solid iron ball, larger than the heavens and the earth. A bird comes once in a hundred millions of years and just touches the great iron ball with a feather of its wing. Think that you have to burn in a fire till the bird has worn the great iron ball away with its feather. Is this eternity? No.

"Think that a man in hell cries only one single tear in ten hundred millions of years. Tell me, how many millions of years must pass before he fills a little basin with his tears? How many millions of years must pass before he cries as many tears as there were drops of water at the Deluge? How many years must pass before he has drowned the heavens and the earth with his tears? Is this eternity? No.

"Turn all the earth into little grains of sand, and fill all the skies and the heavens with little grains of sand. After each hundred millions of years one grain of sand is taken away; oh, what a long, long time it would be before the last grain of sand was taken away. Is this eternity? No.

"Cover all the earth and all the skies with little dots like these ...... Let every dot stand for a hundred thousand millions of years. Is this eternity? No.

3

"After such a long, long time will God still punish sinners? Yes. After all this His anger is not turned away, His hand is still stretched out. How long, then, will the punishment of sinners go on? Forever, and ever, and ever."— *Page 24.*

A doctrine that compels us to have a view of God such as is presented in these extracts should cause us to ponder seriously as to its truthfulness. We stated that the doctrine of the immortal soul had no ground in the Bible. This has been abundantly proved. We also stated that the doctrine in its necessary consequences is unworthy of God, and is a reflection on His character. We have given some of the reasons here for this view. Those who believe in an immortal soul must also believe in an eternal hell and in a god whose wrath never ends. They must believe in endless punishment without purpose, in a punishment not proportionate to the crime, and in a god whose nature is such that it permits him to do what even the basest of men would refuse to do. This is a serious indictment of any doctrine, and should be enough to insure its rejection even apart from its un-Biblical nature.

This leads us to the examination of some doctrines invented for the purpose of escaping the conclusions drawn above. Among these is the doctrine that all mankind will be saved and that of "an intermediate state after death for the expiation of sin"—purgatory. To these we shall now apply ourselves.

# CHAPTER FIVE

# Why an Eternal Hell Is Impossible

THE doctrine of eternal torment is so fearful to contemplate and gives such a dreadful view of God that many are loath to believe it on purely humanitarian grounds. It seems to violate all sense of justice, and changes God from a being of love to one of intense hatred, whose wrath can never be appeased. For this reason many ingenious attempts have been invented to escape the inevitable consequences of a belief in the immortal soul, which underlies the doctrine of eternal hell-fire.

One of these attempts has resulted in the belief that eventually all will be saved. Another is the doctrine of purgatory, which is believed to be an intermediate state where the souls are purified and fitted for heaven. The Universalist doctrine provides for the salvation of all, and thus clears God of the charge of cruelty and of maintaining a place of purposeless punishment throughout eternity. The doctrine of purgatory leaves but a few incorrigible souls in hell, and provides a motive and a purpose for punishing.

Both of these doctrines must, on Biblical grounds, be rejected, for all people will not be saved; nor is any such place as purgatory mentioned in the Scriptures. Even the Roman Catholics admit this, and refer to the apocryphal books for proof of their belief in an intermediate state, knowing that it cannot be found in the canonical part. It is interesting, however, to note the attempt made to provide a solution for the dreadful consequences of the belief in the doctrine of immortality of the soul. It is evident that there must be a felt need of doing this, and so the one does it by saving all, the other by saving the large majority, thus removing at least partly the reproach cast upon God by the doctrine of hell-fire. This brings us to a consideration of what the Bible teaches as to a future judgment and punishment.

In all points touching salvation and duty the Bible is very clear, and on no subject is it clearer than on that of a future judgment. "It is appointed unto men once to die, but after this the judgment," is the plain statement in Hebrews 9:27. "He hath appointed a day, in the which He will judge the world." Acts 17:31. This judgment is necessary. Men here do not always receive their just awards. Some men apparently succeed with their wicked machinations, while others who have pure motives and good intentions are caught in skillfully laid snares, and suffer. This life does not always reward virtue and honesty and punish wickedness. Hence, if justice is to prevail, there must come a day of reckoning. God cannot be God and not have a day of judgment.

But this day of judgment, if it is to take into account the consequences of an act as well as the act itself, cannot come until earthly history is past and all results accounted for. Few are the acts, good or bad, that do not have widespreading consequences that take time for development. They "rest from their labors," the Bible says; "and their works do follow them." Revelation 14:13. Paul lived nineteen centuries ago, but his life and writings still influence men. Tom Paine is moldering in the dust, but his pernicious influence is not dead. Thus, if the judgment is to account for the whole life of man, and if all the factors are to be taken into consideration, not until time finally ceases can a complete record be assembled. It is therefore impossible to have a general judgment at the death of each individual. It must be deferred until "the last day."

With this view the Bible harmonizes. God "hath appointed a day, in the which He will judge." Acts 17:31. In Paul's time that day was still in the future, and is spoken of as "judgment to come." Acts 24:25. The wicked angels are kept "unto the judgment of the great day." Jude 6. In that day Christ will "separate them . . . as a shepherd divideth his sheep from the goats" (Matthew 25:31-34); and this will be in connection with the events of the thousand years, at which time John "saw thrones, and they sat upon them, and judgment was given unto them" (Revelation 20:4). It is after the heavens are departed and the islands and mountains are moved out of their places that "the great day of His wrath" will come. Revelation 6:14-17. At that time John also "saw the dead, small and great, stand before God; and the books were opened: . . . and the dead were judged." Revelation 20:12. With this view of a general judgment day at the end of time the whole Bible agrees.

We now come to another question that must be settled at this time. If the judgment does not take place at death, but at some future time, what happens to those who die? Where are they, and in what condition? It would manifestly be unfair to send them to the place of punishment before their cases have been decided in the judgment, and it would likewise be questionable to send them to heaven to enjoy the bliss of the redeemed only to be afterward called into judgment with the possibility of being sent elsewhere. It would seem imperative to have all cases judged before sending them to one place or the other; and, as this judgment will not take place until the end of the world, what disposition shall be made of the dead until that time? Where are they, and in what condition?

These are embarrassing questions for those who believe in the doctrine of an immortal soul. They must provide in some way for those who have departed this life; and as they, of course, cannot have them die and be at rest until the resurrection morning, they conceive of a kind of judgment at death, after which the soul is sent to one place or the other until the final decision of the last day. This view has the objection that it is thoroughly un-Biblical, and makes entirely unnecessary both the resurrection and the final judg-

ment; for, if a soul is already enjoying eternal bliss in heaven
above, how could there possibly be any need of a resurrection? Indeed, how could one be brought about? And of what
use would it be if it could be accomplished? Would or could
a resurrection be of any possible value to a soul who already
is in heaven? It would seem both unnecessary and useless,
not to say foolish.

Also, of what use would a resurrection be to one who is
already in hell? The soul is there in torment, but suddenly
it gets word that it is going to be resurrected. For what purpose could that possibly be? For the purpose of judgment,
one would answer. But if the soul is already in hell, suffering the agonies of the damned, would it not be mockery to
have it appear before the judgment seat to have the case
tried, to determine the justice of the sentence that has already been in execution for millenniums, perhaps? It would
seem that in such a case justice surely would be turned back-
ward.

What, then, about the dead? We have learned in the preceding chapters that man is mortal, subject to death, and
that immortality is not an inherited condition, but that it
must be sought for, and is attained only by those who are
Christ's. When a man dies, therefore, just what takes place?
Is any part of him alive, or is he really and totally dead?

The spirit, we learned, is the impersonal, life-giving breath
from God, which in the beginning was breathed into the nostrils of Adam and made him a living soul. This "breath of
life" was given to man and beast alike, and is the universal
life principle from God. Genesis 2:7; 7:15, 21, 22. At death
this breath of life goes back to God, who gave it. "The spirit
shall return unto God who gave it." Ecclesiastes 12:7. It
came from God; it goes back to God. It was impersonal
when it was breathed into Adam; it returns the same way.
The spirit, the breath of life, leaves man and beast at death.
God gave them life; now He takes it away. And the life re-

turns to God who gave it. As in the beginning this breath of life caused Adam to become a living soul, so now when it is taken away it leaves the form as it was before—lifeless, inert, without consciousness, without personality. What has become of the soul? It has ceased to be. As the music ceases when the bow is stilled upon the strings, as the light departs when the current is turned off, so the soul—consciousness, personality, will—is no more when God withdraws His spirit. Man then rests in peace until the morning of the resurrection. "He entereth into peace; they rest in their beds, each one that walketh in his uprightness." Isaiah 57:2, R. V.

Death is compared to a sleep. "Many of them that sleep in the dust of the earth shall awake." Daniel 12:2. Stephen "fell asleep." Acts 7:60. Christ is the first fruits of them "that slept." 1 Corinthinas 15:20. We are not to be ignorant of them that "are asleep." 1 Thessalonians 4:13, 14.

In untroubled sleep there is perfect unconsciousness. To all such, time is nonexistent. So also is it in death. Their "thoughts perish." Psalm 146:4. They have "no remembrance." Psalm 6:5. They "cannot praise" God. Isaiah 38:18. "The dead know not anything." Ecclesiastes 9:5. They "go down into silence." Psalm 115:17.

This, then, is man's condition in death. The grave is his house. Job 17:13. There he rests in peace until the call comes. Then "all that are in the graves shall hear His voice, and shall come forth." John 5:28. "Thy dead men shall live, together with my dead body shall they arise." Isaiah 26:19. "The trumpet shall sound, and the dead shall be raised." 1 Corinthians 15:52. "The dead in Christ shall rise first." 1 Thessalonians 4:16.

This Biblical view of man's condition in death makes the resurrection a necessity, and gives point to Paul's word: "If Christ be not raised, your faith is vain. . . . *Then they also which are fallen asleep in Christ are perished.*" 1 Corinthians 15:17, 18. How could those words possibly be true if the doctrine that the righteous at death go immediately to heaven is true? No, the resurrection is a necessity. If it were not for that, they that "are fallen asleep in Christ are perished."

Is it not true, however, that the doctrine that men go directly to heaven at death is a much more beautiful and comforting doctrine than the one that all sleep in peace until the resurrection morning? There would, indeed, be some point to this observation if we were not painfully aware that all do not die possessed of a sure hope of heaven. We fear that a large number die without God and without hope. Where do these go? Would not the thought of this great number going immediately to eternal torment neutralize the joy of knowing that some go immediately to heaven? And would not the certainty of having a large number in torment be a somewhat gloomy doctrine? At least it would not seem to be so much more beautiful and comforting than the Biblical one that all sleep in peace until the day of judgment and reward.

But aside from Biblical considerations, there are weighty reasons why it is best to have all sleep in the grave until the resurrection morning. Some of these reasons we shall now consider.

# CHAPTER SIX

# *Why Not Go to Heaven at Death?*

ORIGINALLY heaven was synonymous with all that pertains to joy and happiness; but when sin reared its ugly head, a note of discord was struck, and sorrow and pain made their entrance even into the courts above.

Was there rejoicing in heaven when Christ hung upon the cross and in agony of soul cried out, "My God, My God, why hast Thou forsaken Me?" Was there joy in heaven when thousands upon thousands of God's martyrs gave their lives at the stake or suffered in dungeons? Was there joy in heaven when the Old Testament prophets were persecuted? When Israel went after strange gods? or when, in the days of Noah, God sent a flood upon the whole earth? And will there be joy in heaven when God's people at last come face to face with "the beast and his image" and go through "the time of Jacob's trouble"? No; not until sin shall be eradicated and sinners be no more will perfect happiness and joy reign supreme.

There cannot be joy and happiness in the very nature of the case, for Jesus is "touched with the feeling of our infirmities" (Hebrews 4:15); He weeps with those that weep (John 11:35); "in all their affliction He was afflicted" (Isaiah 63:9). There is much of truth in the song we sing:

> "There's no place where earthly sorrows
> Are more felt than up in heaven."

It would indeed be sad if God were not sympathetic and considerate, if our sorrows and perplexities did not touch His heart. If He is a God of love, He cannot unfeelingly stand by and see His creatures suffer. He suffers with them. With unutterable love He cries out, "How shall I give thee up, Ephraim? how shall I deliver thee, Israel? . . . *Mine heart is turned within Me."* Hosea 11:8. Stronger expression than this cannot be found. It connotes extreme grief and sorrow on the part of God.

The world has gone through many sad experiences since sin entered, and trial and persecution have been the lot of God's people. There is no sorrow on earth that has not found a responsive chord in heaven. The Father's heart is indeed touched with our grief. When we therefore speak of heaven as a place of joy and happiness, we must qualify that as having reference to the future state, when sin shall be no more. At the present time the statement would not apply.

Heaven is a place of busy activity. Its interests center on this earth—in man's salvation. Angelic messengers are ever on the alert to be of assistance where needed. They are "ministering spirits, sent forth to minister for them who shall be heirs of salvation." Hebrews 1:14. Prayers are continually ascending to God, and angels are dispatched hither and yon in answer to requests for help. An interesting example of this is found in Daniel 9:20-23.

Suppose a soul from earth were suddenly transported to heaven, as is the common belief of those who think the soul immediately goes to glory at death. In what condition would such a soul find itself?

One of two things would be possible: The soul—or as we would prefer to say, the person—could be shut off from all knowledge of the earth and the happenings therein. That, however, would not be ideal; for it is in things here on the earth that all heaven is interested. It is here that Christ lived and died. It is here that the great controversy is being decided. It is here that even right now the struggle between good and evil is being waged to a consummation. And the soul that has just arrived from earth would certainly be interested in knowing how the others he left behind are getting along. To be shut off from any knowledge of the earth would be to live in a state of dreadful suspense.

And the soul, perchance, left father or mother or some near and dear relatives at a critical time in their career. And now he is in heaven, but shut off from any knowledge of things on earth. The angels bring messages continually, prayers are ascending daily, but the newly arrived soul is kept in complete ignorance of what it is all about. Everybody else is busily engaged in helping men still on the earth, but he can have no part therein.

It would seem that such a condition would not be very satisfactory. To be in heaven, where everyone is anxiously interested in men on earth, and yet to be shut out from any participation in the work and plan of salvation; to be kept in ignorance of the progress and fate of those in whom we are vitally interested—husband, wife, daughter, son; to find ourselves surrounded by angels who are busily engaged in helping those for whom we ourselves would gladly lay down our lives, and yet be unable to get any word concerning our loved ones or be permitted to join the busy workers,—this would hardly be an ideal heaven. In fact, many would be tempted to think that they would be better off not to be there.

The other alternative would be to let the newly arrived soul have full access to all the knowledge of earth that heaven possesses. Let him have a part in the work the angels do for man's salvation. Permit him to follow the fortunes of those he left behind. Keep him acquainted with things on earth and how the battle is going. Let him assist in a special way those who by ties of nature are near and dear to him. That surely would seem satisfactory.

And yet, would such a thing be satisfactory after all? Suppose—and this is not an extreme case, either—that a wife and mother died leaving a husband, two daughters, and a son. The home she leaves motherless and wifeless has always been a happy, love-filled, Christian home.

But sudden death takes her away, and—according to the

popular conception—she goes at once to heaven. She is delighted with heaven, but of course her mind is upon her lonely husband and motherless children.

A few months go by, and her husband marries again. The second wife is interested only in spending his money, does not like his children, and lets them go whenever and wherever they wish with no let or hindrance. Soon the boy gets in with wrong companions, engages in petty thievery, and is sent to the state juvenile home. One of the daughters falls in love with a worthless ne'er-do-well, elopes, falsifies her age on a marriage certificate, and begins a life of poverty, with too many children and a husband who eventually deserts her. Instead of finishing her education, the other daughter goes out to work as a waitress in a restaurant. Later she works in a tavern, becomes addicted to drink, and is killed in a drunken-driving accident on the highway at three o'clock in the morning.

All this time the mother, although surrounded by the beauties and felicities of heaven, is frantic over the tragedies in her family on earth. She can do nothing about it, only look on and see it all. To know it all, and yet to be so helpless and powerless, makes heaven a hell for her.

But we need not portray this black picture any further, for it is all fictitious. There is no such thing going on as we have imagined, for those who depart this life rest peacefully and unconsciously in their graves until the day of the great resurrection. God knows best. He knows that any other way for the dead would only result in misery for millions of the departed. So all, saint and sinner alike, sleep until the resurrection morning. Then when all things are ready, when sin is finally done, He will call forth the righteous dead. Then all tears shall be wiped away, and sorrow and pain shall be no more.

How much better God's plan is than man's! It would not do for God to transport souls directly to heaven at death.

Such souls would be in misery if they knew of conditions on earth, yet were unable to help; and they would be in misery if they were kept in ignorance. In either case heaven would cease to be heaven to them. God therefore "giveth His beloved sleep." Sweetly they rest until they hear the voice of the Archangel calling them. 1 Thessalonians 4:16. And when they are called, the work is finished. It is better so.

There is a divine harmony in all that God does. It would seem awkward, to say the least, to have some kind of judgment at death and send people to heaven or hell immediately, and then afterward have a resurrection and a judgment. Why a resurrection and a judgment when their cases are already decided, and they are in the place assigned to them? Why should a soul who is already in heaven, who has "shuffled off this mortal coil" and is enjoying freedom from hampering bodily restrictions, be asked to come down to this earth and have a resurrection and be put into a body again? Can there be any possible reason for a resurrection under such conditions? A resurrection would seem not only superfluous but a positive detriment. Yet such absurdities are inherent in the doctrine of natural immortality.

It is not the intention to leave the impression that heaven is a place of anxiety and sorrow only. There is joy in heaven over one sinner that repents. And there are many that repent. But, conversely, there is also sorrow over the many who do not repent. The same Christ who wept over Jerusalem is now weeping over our small and large cities. Yes, there is sorrow in heaven. There is weeping. And as we come to the last great crisis, the intensity increases. It is just as well that those who are laid to rest really rest "until the indignation be overpast." That is God's plan, and it is best.

We hold, then, to the Biblical doctrine of immortality in Christ only; that those who are His will gain immortality and life through Christ, and that those who are lost will be punished according to the deeds done in the body; that all, whether good or wicked, sleep quietly until the resurrection, and that then the great and final separation takes place. It now behooves us to consider the judgment to come, and how it will do its work. Who will be the judge or judges? and how will the work be carried on?

# CHAPTER SEVEN

# Will God Give Us a Fair Trial?

WHAT about the judgment to come? Will there be one? Who will be the judge or judges, and how will justice be administered?

We have already considered the necessity of a judgment. If virtue is better than vice, if right conduct is preferable to wrong actions, then sometime, somewhere, there should be a recognition of that fact by the God of the universe. Right conduct is not always rewarded here on earth, nor is vice always punished. But if sin breeds suffering and death, and if virtue and good conduct are conducive to happiness and long life, God must in some way step in and demonstrate it. A judgment is necessary, and a judgment day is coming.

God must be just. This is essential and fundamental. And God's justice must be such as to be comprehensible by man. Being made in the image of God includes an intellectual likeness. Our notions of right and wrong and just deserts for transgressions are reflections of God's ideas on the same subjects. Men believe that there must be some relation between transgression and penalty for transgression. Our sense of justice forbids us to mete out the same punishment for the infraction of a police regulation—such as overtime parking—as for the crime of kidnaping. Walking on the grass when there is a sign forbidding it is a violation of law, but is not to be compared with highway robbery. A boy who has broken a neighbor's window may require attention, but no one would treat him as he would a hardened transgressor of the narcotic law. Men make a difference, and fit the punishment to the crime. This appears to them just, and is evidently in harmony with the mind of God.

If God's judgment is to be just, we would expect that all the factors bearing on each case would be considered. It would not be just to present one side only and leave other vital matters out of consideration. For the sake of justice, therefore, it is comforting to know that God will "bring every work into judgment, *with every secret thing, whether it be good, or whether it be evil.*" Ecclesiastes 12:14. This assures us that nothing bearing on the case, "whether it be good, or whether it be evil," will be left out. There will be no covering up of testimony. If there are any extenuating circumstances, they will be considered. This approaches ideal justice.

If the ends of justice are to be served, the testimony given must be unimpeachable. Men sometimes forget. Time effaces the distinctness of an event. May we be sure that in God's court there is no miscarriage of justice because of faulty memory or biased opinion?

From the Bible it appears that nothing is left to the chance of memory alone, though we suppose that none would doubt the accuracy of angelic testimony. "The dead were judged out of those things which were written in the books." Revelation 20:12. Apparently a faithful record is made of each life, and every transaction is truthfully recorded. "Every idle word that men shall speak, they shall give account thereof in the day of judgment." Matthew 12:36. If we are to give an account of every word, and if we are to be judged out of those things that are "written in the books," it follows that our words are written in the books.

This harmonizes with the statement in Malachi 3:16 concerning the righteous, that "the Lord hearkened, and heard it, and a book of remembrance was written." The words are recorded as they are spoken, and this written record is produced in the judgment. That makes the matter sure. There is no doubt as to the testimony. And to make the matter doubly sure, the individuals under sentence agree with the written record, "their conscience also bearing witness, and their thoughts the meanwhile accusing or else excusing one

another, in the day when God shall judge the secrets of men."
Romans 2:15, 16. This phase of the judgment also seems
ideal. Not only are all circumstances taken into consideration, and the testimony presented full and complete, but it
is also authentic and authoritative, and is accepted as such
by the accused.

One more consideration may be pertinent. Is the presiding Judge fair and impartial? Is He competent? Is He
harsh and exacting, or does He tend toward mercy?

For certain reasons God the Father is not the judge, but
has "committed all judgment unto the Son." John 5:22.
See also Acts 10:42; 17:31. This is both interesting and
important. The Father is competent, He is just, He is righteous. But He has never been identified with man as Jesus
has; and this apparently is one reason for the selection of
Christ as judge. The Father has given Christ "authority to
execute judgment also, *because He is the Son of man.*"
Verse 27.

To be sure, the preceding paragraph must be understood
in the light of the two judgments—the investigative and the
executive. In the investigative judgment, which is going on
now in the courts above, God the Father is the judge and
Jesus Christ is our advocate. But in the executive judgment, which comes during the millennial period after Christ's
second coming, Christ is the judge who metes out the sentences.

As man, Christ came to this world and "was in all points
tempted like as we are;" hence He can "be touched with the
feeling of our infirmities." Hebrews 4:15. In Christ we have
One who understands all the sorrows and perplexities of
man, because He has been a man Himself. He is of our
flesh and blood; He is the Son of man, and is "touched with
the feeling of our infirmities." In all the universe there could
be no one else so well fitted for the position of judge, and
none other to whom we could so confidently commit our case.

4

But God has gone one step further in assuring men of a perfectly fair and sympathetic trial. While Christ is the chief presiding judge, He is not the only judge. Associated with Him on the bench are the saints of God, saved through grace. "Do ye not know that the saints shall judge the world?" 1 Corinthians 6:2. "Judgment was given to the saints of the Most High." Daniel 7:22. And so Christ Himself stated of the twelve: "When the Son of man shall sit in the throne of His glory, ye also shall sit upon twelve thrones, judging the twelve tribes of Israel." Matthew 19:28.

These statements make clear the fact that the saints will have a part in the judgment. They will "judge the world." And even beyond the world will their jurisdiction extend. "Know ye not that we shall judge angels?" 1 Corinthians 6:3. When the final assize is held, the saints will have a prominent part to play. Christ associates them with Himself. They hear all the evidence. They are made acquainted with all the circumstances. And when at last the irrevocable decree is pronounced, they are assured of its justice and are able to exclaim from a personal knowledge of the facts involved: "True and righteous are Thy judgments." Revelation 16:7; 19:2. And the angel of the waters confirms this opinion by saying, "Thou art righteous, O Lord, which art, and wast, and shalt be, because Thou hast judged thus." Revelation 16:5.

That Christ thus associates the saints with Himself in the judgment reveals one of the working principles of God's government that is very interesting indeed. God could do all the judging Himself were He so inclined. In a moment He could decide every case, and it would be a just decision. But God does not work that way. He always gives man something to do, thus making him a co-worker with Himself. Christ may raise Lazarus from the dead. Man cannot do that, but man can roll away the stone that covers the grave. Hence Christ commands, "Take *ye* away the stone." John

11:39. Lazarus is called to life, but the bandages are not removed. That man can do; hence Christ again commands, "Loose him, and let him go." Verse 44. The principle here seems to be this, Whatever man can do, let man do. What man cannot do, God will.

But there are other reasons for God's taking man into partnership. In the case of Lazarus here referred to, no doubt was ever afterward expressed by anyone as to the genuineness of the miracle. When those men loosed Lazarus from his graveclothes, when they actually untied the bands that held his hands and feet, and uncovered his face, they were confronted by a miracle other than that of raising a man from the dead. Had they not seen Lazarus come "forth, bound hand and foot with graveclothes"? And how could a man walk when he was bound hand and foot? Yet they had seen him come forth. He had not walked. He could not, for he was bound. Yet he "came forth." And they themselves had untied the bands; so they knew he had been bound. Here was indeed a miracle of which they never tired of telling. These Jews had had a part in this wonderful event, and that constituted them witnesses in its favor. All this testimony would have been lost, had they not been permitted to co-operate.

So in the judgment. God is abundantly able to do all that is to be done without our help. But it is better that we have a part in it. No question can then ever be raised as to God's justice. It is conceivable that some will be lost whom we rather expected would be saved. If we ourselves have heard the case, if we are acquainted with all the circumstances, no doubt will ever arise in our minds as to the justice of the decision. That is forestalled by taking us into partnership. We need never be in doubt as to any decision. *We know.* We sat on the case.

It may be worth while to notice in passing that this principle is one of the things that will make life in the hereafter worth while. We shall not be mere spectators. We shall have a part in God's government and plan. Life would be unendurable were we forever to be "outsiders," or to be treated as children incapable of understanding or of having a part with God.

We are now ready for court to open. We have as presiding judge One who is competent and understanding. He has been man Himself. He has stood before a corrupt human court, and been condemned to death on false testimony. He knows what it is to be arraigned before a weak or biased judge. He has been confronted with lying and suborned witnesses. He knows what it is to have His words given a perverted meaning and an unintended slant. And He is there to see that no such thing is done here, that absolute and impartial justice will be meted out. Associated with Him are the saints. They also have had an experience. They have been tempted, and have fallen. They know the wiles of the evil one, and how craftily his snares have been laid. They have been saved by grace, and their hearts are filled with love and praise to God and with sympathy for those who at last are to be lost. From a court such as this we may expect not only fairness and justice, but also the assurance that the final decree will be in accord with their innate sense of right.

We have noticed before that justice demands that any punishment meted out shall be proportionate to the crime. This principle is accepted and emphasized in the Bible. Man is to be judged "according to his works;" "according to his ways;" "according to the fruit of his doings;" "according to his deeds;" "according as his work shall be." Matthew 16: 27; Jeremiah 17:10; 32:19; Romans 2:6; Revelation 22:12. Hence, "that servant, which knew his Lord's will, and prepared not himself, neither did according to His will, shall be beaten with many stripes. But he that knew not, and did commit things worthy of stripes, shall be beaten with few stripes." Luke 12:47, 48. This seems right and in accordance with ordinary rules of justice. The application of this principle would, of course, preclude any wholesale condemnation of souls to the tortures of hell. It would, however, call for careful investigation that exact justice be done.

The gospel offers men life. "I am come," Christ says, "that they might have life, and that they might have it more abundantly." John 10:10. This is the very essence of the message from heaven. God "gave His only-begotten Son, that whosoever believeth in Him should not perish, but have everlasting life." John 3:16. When men reject this offer, they reject Heaven's choicest gift. To be deprived of life is the greatest punishment that can come to anyone, for with life goes everything else. And it is to save men from perishing that God sent His Son. Those who do not accept Him will eventually perish.

The life we here live is given us that we may decide whether we care to live on and become partakers of the more abundant life that Christ came to give or whether we do not care to make the effort to comply with the conditions of eternal life. We get a little taste of life here, and realize by contrast what it might be if sin and sorrow were excluded. Do we care for life? There are many pleasant things here—love, friendship, and social adventure. There are also many unpleasant things—sorrow, pain, and disappointment. God offers to take out of life all that offends, and to fill it full of good things far beyond our powers even to comprehend, and asks us if we will accept such an offer. There are certain conditions attached to it, but only such as are necessary in the very nature of the case. Will we comply with these conditions? Those who do, receive eternal life.

The judgment of which we speak concerns those who have rejected God's offer of life. They have in reality already settled their own cases. Life has been offered them. They have rejected it. They have judged themselves "unworthy of everlasting life." Acts 13:46. They have come short, they have sinned, and they are now about to receive the wages of sin, death. Romans 6:23.

In speaking of the final punishment of the wicked as being death, we are well aware that some punishment must precede the final sentence. There must be consideration given to the deeds done in the body, and just deserts must be administered. He who knowingly has done wickedly must be beaten with "many stripes." He who unwittingly did evil will escape with "few stripes." In the end, however,—and here is where we must disagree with those who believe in endless punishment,—"the wages of sin is death," death eternal and everlasting. This is at once the hardest, the most merciful, and the most just, sentence. To this particular phase of the subject we shall now give our attention.

# CHAPTER EIGHT

# We Reject Eternal Torment

MANY religionists believe that the wicked will exist forever in endless tortures in hell. The statements in the Bible that the wicked shall perish, that they shall die and be no more, they interpret to mean something else. Are they justified in their views and in their interpretations? Is there any foundation for this belief?

Let us first of all notice just what the Bible says in regard to the fate of the wicked.

*They shall perish.* "God so loved the world, that He gave His only-begotten Son, that whosoever believeth in Him should not *perish,* but have everlasting life." John 3:16. See also John 10:28; Romans 2:12; Psalms 37:20; 92:9. *To perish* is defined: To pass away from life or existence; to be destroyed; to come to nothing; to waste away; to pass away; to die.

*They shall be destroyed.* "The Lord preserveth all them that love Him: but all the wicked will He destroy." Psalm 145:20. See also Psalm 92:7; Proverbs 29:1; Luke 17:27-29; 1 Thessalonians 5:3; 2 Thessalonians 2:8, 9; Philippians 3:19. *To destroy* is defined: To unbuild; to break up the structure and organic existence of; to demolish; to ruin, to bring to nought; to put an end to; to kill, to slay.

*They shall die.* "The soul that sinneth, it shall die." Ezekiel 18:4. See also Ezekiel 18:26; Romans 8:13; 6:23; James 1:15; Revelation 21:8. *To die* is defined: To cease to live; to become dead; to perish; to pass away from life; to expire; to cease to exist.

*They shall be cut off.* "The Lord loveth judgment, and forsaketh not His saints; they are preserved forever: but the seed of the wicked shall be cut off." Psalm 37:28. See also Psalms 37:22, 38; 94:23; Proverbs 2:22; 1 Samuel 28:9.

_Cut off_ is defined: To put an end to; to destroy; to cause to die an untimely death.

_They shall be slain._ "Those Mine enemies, which would not that I should reign over them, bring hither, and _slay_ them before Me." Luke 19:27. See also Isaiah 11:4; Psalm 34:21. _Slay_ is defined: To kill; to put to death by violence; to destroy.

_They shall be consumed._ "The wicked ... shall _consume;_ into smoke shall they _consume_ away." Psalm 37:20. See also 2 Thessalonians 2:8; Deuteronomy 32:22; Isaiah 5:24; Psalm 104:35. _Consume_ is defined: To destroy gradually, as by burning or decomposition; to use up.

_They shall be no more._ "For yet a little while, and the wicked _shall not be._" Psalm 37:10. "Let the sinners be consumed out of the earth, and let the wicked _be no more._" Psalm 104:35. "They shall be as though they _had not been._" Obadiah 16.

_They shall be rooted out._ "The wicked shall be cut off from the earth, and the transgressors shall be _rooted out of it._" Proverbs 2:22. See also Psalm 52:5; Isaiah 5:24; Malachi 4:1. _Root out_ is defined: To pull, dig, or tear up by the roots; to eradicate; to extirpate.

_They shall be despoiled of life._ Proverbs 22:23, R. V.

They shall be _burned up._ Psalm 97:3; Matthew 3:12.

They shall _become ashes._ Malachi 4:3.

They shall _become as smoke._ Psalm 37:20.

They shall be _cast away_, as bad fish. Matthew 13:48.

It would seem from these passages that God intends to convey the idea that the time will come when the wicked shall be no more. He is at pains to select words and illustrations that imply not only cessation of life and activity but annihilation. And it may be interesting to know that God selects the strongest words that can be found to convey His thoughts in this subject. The wicked shall not only "burn," for which the Greek word is _"kaio,"_ but they shall "burn up," a much stronger word, *"katakaio."* Luke 3:17; Matthew 3:12; Psalm 97:3. In like manner they shall not only be "destroyed," but "utterly destroyed," a much stronger expression. Acts 3:23, R. V. It is not merely the ordinary word "consume" that is used, but "consume away." Psalm 37:20. Again it is not enough for them to "perish." They shall "utterly perish." 2 Peter 2:12. They shall not merely be "eaten" by the moths, but "eaten up," "devoured." Isaiah 51:8; Revelation 20:9.

If it were said of a person that he had died, had been despoiled of life, had been slain; that he was utterly destroyed, burned up, consumed; had become as ashes; had become as smoke; had ceased to exist as completely as though he had never been,—if all this were said, it would certainly seem to indicate that the one saying it meant to convey the idea that the man was dead, and not in possession of life. If this is not the meaning of the words, we would be at a loss how to convey any thought by means of words.

Now, all these phrases are used of those upon whom God's wrath will finally rest. They and many others of similar import are used over and over again. From all these expressions we can draw but one conclusion: "The wages of sin is death;" therefore the wicked will not live forever, but will at last cease to exist.

Why should men cling to the belief that there will be an eternally burning hell-fire? It is not that anyone would wish it so; for the thought that many will spend eternity cursing God in torment can certainly not be a pleasing one. Men would far rather that it were otherwise; but they cannot escape the logic of their own belief. If men have immortal souls, they cannot die. As only a minority is saved, and as the others cannot die, they must be consigned to some place —and the only other place is hell, unless one invents a purgatory. The doctrine of the immortality of the soul inevitably leads to a belief in eternal hell-fire and eternal torment.

It has been conclusively proved in these chapters that men are not possessed of immortal souls. Immortality is had only through Christ. And with the fall of the doctrine of natural immortality goes also a belief in eternal hell-fire; the one is dependent on the other. If men do not have immortal souls, they cannot live forever, in hell or anywhere else. If they are so to live, it must be a gift from God. And that is just what the Bible says. "The wages of sin is death; but *the gift of God is eternal life* through Jesus Christ our Lord." Romans 6:23. This gift God will give to His own, but He will not give it to the wicked. If He should give it to them, it would merely condemn them to a life of suffering. And that would hardly be a gift. How much better is God's plan! "He that hath the Son hath life; and he that hath not the Son of God hath not life." 1 John 5:12. *"No murderer hath eternal life abiding in him."* 1 John 3:15. If these statements are true, eternal hell-fire ceases to be a fact.

We reject the doctrine of eternal torment on the ground that the saints who will have part in the judgment could never condemn their fellow creatures to unending torture. Their sense of justice would not permit them to do so.

We reject the doctrine of eternal torment on the ground that it provides a punishment altogether out of proportion to the crime, and thus violates all rules of right.

We reject the doctrine of eternal torment because it is irreconcilable with the picture that the Bible gives us of Christ. The Christ who took the little children in His arms and blessed them while here on earth will not take other little children and burn them throughout eternity. We may accept one Christ or the other, but we cannot accept both.

We reject the doctrine of eternal torment because it robs us of our God of love, and substitutes a being whose wrath is never appeased.

We reject the doctrine of eternal torment because it provides for a plague spot in God's universe throughout all eternity, and makes it impossible for God Himself ever to abolish it.

We reject the doctrine of eternal torment because it perpetuates and immortalizes sin, suffering, and sorrow, and thus contradicts and nullifies God's statement that the time will come when these shall no more exist. Revelation 21:4.

We reject the doctrine of eternal torment because it would forever cast a shadow over the joy of the redeemed to know that somewhere in the universe blood of their own blood and flesh of their own flesh were in torment.

We reject the doctrine of eternal torment because it vilifies God's character and limits His power, in that it either presents Him as perpetuating torment because it accords with His character, and as willing miraculously to sustain life in the unhappy victims for the purpose of aimless and endless punishment—or else as powerless to stop that of which He does not approve.

We reject the doctrine of eternal torment because of the fruit it has brought forth here on earth. If God can torture men throughout eternity and cause them to pass through excruciating agony, may not men in their limited way follow His example? Indeed, if men, in torturing their fellow creatures for their faith, could save them from the fiercer wrath of God, would they not be doing a meritorious deed? The Inquisition was not always carried on by bloodthirsty men. To the contrary, many of them were sincere men, who thought they were doing the will of God. They were firm in the belief that heretics were doomed to suffer the eternal vengeance of God, and they were anxious to save souls.

But many of these heretics were stubborn, and did not want to be saved. What could be done? According to popular doctrine, heretics would fall into the hands of an angry God, and eternal suffering would be their lot. But it might be possible to get some of them to accept the orthodox faith if sufficient pressure were brought to bear on them. What if they were burned over a slow fire, which, at most, would last but a few hours, and their suffering then be at an end, if by this means they would escape the greater torture that would be theirs if they died in their heresy and were sent to eternal torment? If burning them an hour would save their burning an eternity, would not the lesser punishment be an act of mercy rather than a horrible tragedy? So reasoned these men, and on these grounds they justify the Inquisition. The deluge of blood that has engulfed this world through the Inquisition; the indescribable tortures suffered in dungeons and at the stake; the terror that reigned through the ages when men suffered for their faith; the reflex influence that this had on the persecutors; the tears and heart-rending agonies suffered by the saints of God; the perverted picture men were given of God,—all is traceable to the influence of the doctrine of eternal torment. Because of the fruit of this doctrine we reject it.

Finally, we reject the doctrine of eternal torment because it is unscriptural; because it is based on the doctrine of the immortality of the soul, which is also unscriptural and the father of spiritism, transmigration of the soul, purgatory, and a host of other errors.

# CHAPTER NINE

# The Rich Man and Lazarus

THIS study would not be complete without some consideration being given to objections sometimes urged against the views here presented. Are there not statements in the Bible which indicate that the punishment of the wicked will ever continue, that it is eternal in its nature? Does not the story of the rich man and Lazarus teach that men at death go to their eternal home,—some to heaven and others to the place of torment?

We shall first consider the narrative of the rich man and Lazarus as recorded in Luke 16:19-31. "There was a certain rich man, which was clothed in purple and fine linen, and fared sumptuously every day: and there was a certain beggar named Lazarus, which was laid at his gate, full of sores, and desiring to be fed with the crumbs which fell from the rich man's table: moreover the dogs came and licked his sores. And it came to pass, that the beggar died, and was carried by the angels into Abraham's bosom: the rich man also died, and was buried; and in hell he lift up his eyes, being in torments, and seeth Abraham afar off, and Lazarus in his bosom. And he cried and said, Father Abraham, have mercy on me, and send Lazarus, that he may dip the tip of his finger in water, and cool my tongue; for I am tormented in this flame. But Abraham said, Son, remember that thou in thy lifetime receivedst thy good things, and likewise Lazarus evil things: but now he is comforted, and thou art tormented. And beside all this, between us and you there is a great gulf fixed: so that they which would pass from hence to you cannot; neither can they pass to us, that would come from thence. Then he said, I pray thee therefore, father, that thou wouldest send him to my father's house: for I have five brethren; that he may testify unto them, lest they also come into this place of torment. Abraham saith unto him, They have Moses and the prophets; let them hear them. And he said, Nay, father Abraham: but if one went unto them from the dead, they will repent. And he said unto him, If they hear not Moses and the prophets, neither will they be persuaded, though one rose from the dead."

This parable connects in thought closely with that of the unjust steward in the same chapter, verses 1 to 12, the intervening verses, 13 to 18, being largely comments by Christ on the attitude of the Pharisees who derided Him. The Lord had commended the wisdom of the unjust steward who, when he was called to give an account of his stewardship and was about to lose his position, had said to the man who owed his lord a hundred measures of oil, "Take thy bill, and sit down quickly, and write fifty." To another, who owed a hundred measures of wheat, he had said: "Take thy bill, and write fourscore." Verses 6, 7. These men would thus be under obligation to the steward, and would probably help him should he be discharged. If they did not do so, the steward might expose them; and thus they would be compelled to pay the full amount.

This parable illustrates one principle that always should be kept in mind when interpreting the parabolic teachings of the Bible. This principle may be expressed thus: Each parable has one main object or lesson. Beware of drawing an unwarranted conclusion from incidental happenings in a parable which are introduced merely to complete the picture, but have no bearing on the main subject or lesson to be taught. This lesson stands out clearly, and need not be misunderstood. To give the lesson its proper setting, other features may be brought in, which do not affect the main lesson but merely serve to complete the picture. The careful student must discriminate between the chief lesson and the minor details, lest confusion result.

In the parable of the unjust steward "the Lord com-

mended the unjust steward, because he had done wisely."
Verse 8. The facts revealed in the parable show that the
steward had been dishonest. Does the Lord commend dis-
honesty? Anyone drawing such a conclusion would certainly thereby reveal his lack of comprehension of spiritual
things. Rather the lesson is clear: The unjust steward had
provided for his future. He had made sure that he had
friends who would take care of him when he was dismissed
from his position. He had done wisely in this; and this wisdom the Lord commends even though He could not approve
of the methods used.

Applying this parable spiritually: Have we made provision for the future? Are we sure that we have used our
means in a way to make "friends of the mammon of unrighteousness;" that, when we fail, they may receive us "into
everlasting habitations"? Verse 9.

The Pharisees, "who were covetous, heard all these things:
and they derided Him." Verse 14. For their sakes Christ
spoke another parable,—one also dealing with a rich man,
the same as the parable of the unjust steward,—and showed
what happens to a man who has not provided for the future.
This rich man has all he wants, while the poor man has
nothing. Both die. The rich man suddenly finds himself in
torment, while the poor man is in comfort. The rich man
pleads for himself, but receives no help. He asks that Lazarus may be sent to him with but a drop of water to cool his
tongue, but is told that there is a great gulf fixed, which it
is impossible for man to pass. May Lazarus not, then, be
sent to his brothers, to warn them lest they come into the
same place? No, they would not hear Lazarus though he
should be sent from the dead. They have Moses and the
prophets. Let them hear them.

What, now, is the lesson or the lessons which we may
rightly draw from this parable? The rich man is not presented to us as a great sinner. He is not said to be voluptuous

or unjust. It is not intimated that he got his money unfairly. It does not seem to be Christ's intent to portray him as being specially wicked.

Likewise nothing is said of the character of the poor man. Was he a good man? Was he evil? The parable does not state. We may draw the conclusion that he was a righteous man, and we would probably be right. But apparently Christ did not intend in this parable to discuss the characters of the individuals mentioned. Yet the great commentator De Wette maintains that the only meaning of the parable is: "Woe to the rich; blessed are the poor." Rich men go to hell because they are rich; poor men are saved because they are poor. Such we take to be an utter perversion of the meaning of the parable. Yet equally foolish conclusions must such arrive at who expect to find an application for each part of a parable regardless of the main intent of the lesson. Let the statement be reiterated: Each parable has one main lesson and intent. All minor details incident to the story fill their purpose in rounding out the narrative, and have no bearing on the chief lesson to be inculcated.

What, then, is the lesson of the rich man and Lazarus? That the dead are alive and conscious? That heaven and hell are so close together that men can see one another and converse together? That Abraham's bosom is of such large capacity that it can hold all the poor people who die? That rich men go to hell? That poor people go to heaven? Few persons, we suppose, would draw any such conclusions. Yet such conclusions _might_ be drawn were we to forget the universally admitted principle of parable exegesis: Each parable holds one main lesson, and only one. What, then, is the lesson of the rich man and Lazarus?

To get this clearly in mind, remember the parable of the unjust steward. He had made provision for the future, and God commended his wisdom. The rich man in the parable of Luke 16:19-31 had made no such provision. He had riches; but he had not made friends with his riches. When he died, he was alone. Rich he was in this world's goods; but that did not help him. Christ's advice had been, "Make to yourselves friends of the mammon of unrighteousness; that, when ye fail, they may receive you into everlasting habitations." Luke 16:9.

This, of course, has reference to the future immortal life. We are so to use the talents God has given us—our time, our money, our gifts—that when we fail, they, the angels, may receive us "into everlasting habitations." This the rich man had neglected to do. He had fared sumptuously himself, but had failed to provide for the time when he should "fail." Now, when it was too late, he found "a great gulf fixed: so that they which would pass from hence to you cannot; neither can they pass to us, that would come from thence." Verse 26.

The lesson, therefore, seems to be this: Prepare now for the future. Use God's gifts so as to make friends with them. When death comes, the eternal destiny of souls is fixed. No one can pass from one side to the other. Life's decision is final. There is no second probation. The gulf is so great that no man can pass it. Therefore, prepare now to meet your God.

This is the great lesson of the parable. To contend that its intent is to teach consciousness in death seems altogether irrelevant. How otherwise could Christ present in as striking a way the futility of depending on riches here to carry one through to the kingdom? The rich man was used to being the commander. So in hell he commands: "Send Lazarus." But Lazarus is not sent. Christ is trying to convey to the Pharisees the idea that it is the *use* that is made of money, not its possession, that counts. If the rich man had made friends by the generous use of his money while here on earth, Abraham would have received him into his bosom. But, he had failed. Now it was too late.

5

But, some may object, does not the parable represent the
rich man and Lazarus as alive and speaking? It most certainly does. But how can any story be told unless the characters in the story are made to speak? Note this parable
taken from Judges 9:8-15: "The trees went forth on a time
to anoint a king over them; and they said unto the olive
tree, Reign thou over us. But the olive tree said unto them,
Should I leave my fatness, wherewith by me they honor God
and man, and go to be promoted over the trees? And the
trees said to the fig tree, Come thou, and reign over us. But
the fig tree said unto them, Should I forsake my sweetness,
and my good fruit, and go to be promoted over the trees?
Then said the trees unto the vine, Come thou, and reign
over us. And the vine said unto them, Should I leave my
wine, which cheereth God and man, and go to be promoted
over the trees? Then said all the trees unto the bramble,
Come thou, and reign over us. And the bramble said unto
the trees, If in truth ye anoint me king over you, then come
and put your trust in my shadow: and if not, let fire come
out of the bramble, and devour the cedars of Lebanon."

No one, we suppose, would use this parable as proof that
trees can speak and do the other things here mentioned. Yet,
if anyone should insist that this is part of the Bible, and
that the Bible must be true, and hence trees can speak, we
would not be disposed to argue with them. A mind capable
of such reasoning had better be left alone. We know that
God can make trees and dead people speak should He so
desire; but the fact that they are so presented in a parable
does not make the proposition true in general that all trees
can speak and that all dead people are alive and conscious.

Yet that is what some would make the parable of the rich
man and Lazarus teach. Let the principle before stated be
stressed: A parable is given to teach one main lesson, and
only one. All minor illustrations used are merely to give
point to the lesson.

# CHAPTER TEN

# Will Sinners Live Forever?

IN THIS chapter we shall answer some other objections that are frequently made to the doctrine that men have life only in Christ, that the righteous are saved with an everlasting salvation and will ever be with the Lord, while the wicked will be destroyed after having received their punishment, and that at last they will be no more. One text much quoted by the champions of eternal torment is found in Matthew 25:46: "These shall go away into everlasting punishment: but the righteous into life eternal."

It might be noted here that the words "everlasting" and "eternal" are from the same word in the original, and hence mean the same. As the one is eternal, so is the other. There is no difference. We not only admit this, we stress it. The righteous go into life eternal, the wicked into everlasting punishment.

We have before noted the reward of the righteous. They shall live forever. They shall ever be with the Lord. As long as eternity, as long as God exists, they shall live. The gift of God is everlasting life. God's children shall never cease to be. Their existence is unending.

In like manner the punishment of the wicked is everlasting. It will never cease. It is eternal in its nature. It will last as long as the righteous are in heaven. As everlasting life is predicated of the righteous, so everlasting punishment is predicated of the wicked. The life of the righteous and the punishment of the wicked are equally long. The text states this clearly.

The question that now concerns us is the nature of the punishment of the wicked. We need only remind our readers of what has been said before on this subject. The Bible definitely declares that "the wages of sin is death." Romans

6:23. "The soul that sinneth, it shall die." Ezekiel 18:4. God placed cherubim at the east of the Garden of Eden, "to keep the way of the tree of life," lest man "put forth his hand, and take also of the tree of life, and eat, and live forever." Genesis 3:24, 22. We know that no murderer, no sinner, "hath eternal life abiding in him." 1 John 3:15. It is only he that has the Son that has life; "he that hath not the Son of God hath not life." 1 John 5:12.

Let these scriptures have their God-intended weight. If a soul sins, it shall die. "The wages of sin is death." God evidently means what He says. If life means life, by the same token death means death. Death is the opposite of life, and life is the opposite of death. If the righteous live, the wicked die. They do not both live; they do not both die. One lives and the other dies. The one gets a reward, and the other gets punishment. The reward is life; the punishment is death. And one is as everlasting as the other. The death of the wicked lasts as long as the life of the righteous. Neither has any end.

If any should say that death here does not mean death, that the wicked are not dead but are alive and in conscious torture, we would answer that by the same reasoning the righteous are not alive but dead and in unconscious happiness. If death does not mean death, why should life mean life? If anyone, therefore, should say that when the Bible states that the wicked shall die it does not mean that they really will die, we would maintain that when it says the righteous shall have life it does not really mean life. But would not such be a gross perversion of the Scriptures? We maintain that when the Scriptures promise life to those that are in Christ, the life promised is not death. Likewise, we believe that when the sinner is promised death, death is not life. To confuse life and death, to make the one mean the other, is to confuse God's word and make it of none effect.

God does not wish the sinner to live forever. In the very

beginning, after the fall of man, God placed cherubim to guard the way to the tree of life lest man should eat of it and "live forever." Did man pass the barrier? Have sinners thrust aside the cherubim that God placed there? There is only one way of gaining access to that tree, and that way is Christ. Through Him only can eternal life be had. Hence "he that hath the Son hath life" (1 John 5:12); and yet some would have us believe that God did not guard the way as He intended, but that sinners without Christ have passed the barrier of cherubim and eaten of the tree of life, and hence will live forever. We utterly reject any such God-dishonoring doctrine. God *did* guard the way to the tree of life. Only through Christ can admittance be had. No sinner "hath eternal life abiding in him."

We hold, therefore, to the Biblical doctrine that "the wages of sin is death;" that death is not life, but the opposite of life, the absence of it. We hold that this death is eternal; it is everlasting; it never ends. When the final decree is passed upon the impenitent wicked, they shall at last suffer the loss of that which they have rejected,—life. They have scorned life; they have misused this most precious gift; they have not appreciated it or its opportunities. Now death shall be their portion.

There are a few more texts that it may be well for us to consider at this time. "Depart from Me, ye cursed, into everlasting fire, prepared for the devil and his angels." Matthew 25:41. "If thy hand offend thee, cut it off: it is better for thee to enter into life maimed, than having two hands to go into hell, into the fire that never shall be quenched: where their worm dieth not, and the fire is not quenched." Mark 9:43, 44.

It will be noted here that the statements are very definite—"everlasting fire" and "the fire that never shall be quenched." Just what do these expressions mean? We would answer unhesitatingly, "Exactly what they say."

The word here translated "hell" is taken from the Greek word "Gehenna." This was a valley situated south of Jerusalem, in olden times polluted by the worship of Moloch, and afterward used for a place where the dead bodies of animals and of malefactors were thrown. That these decaying and rotting bodies might not pollute the air and cause pestilence, a fire was kept burning day and night. If such a place of destruction had not been provided, rotting carcasses by the score and by the hundreds would cause sickness and death. As noted above, a place of this kind was in existence just south of Jerusalem, and was called "Gehenna."

Christ was, therefore, using an expression with which the Jews were well acquainted. The Gehenna fires were always burning, and smoke ascending. Carcasses were always rotting there, and worms feeding on them.

This, indeed, is not a very pleasing picture, but certainly most expressive and definite. The Gehenna outside Jerusalem was not used for torturing either living men or animals. It was only dead bodies that were thrown there. This makes the parallel complete, for it is "the carcasses of the men that have transgressed against" the Lord that "shall be an abhorring unto all flesh." Isaiah 66:24. Men who have misused their privileges and wasted their opportunities, and have not appreciated the life that God so graciously has bestowed upon them will at last be thrown aside as worthless material, and consumed.

"Their worm shall not die, neither shall their fire be quenched." Isaiah 66:24. It does not say that their soul shall not die, nor their bodies, but merely that their *worm* shall not die. This worm has a close connection with the word "carcass" used in the same text. It denotes utter destruction. Putrefaction soon begins in a dead carcass. Unless that putrefaction should in some way be arrested, the carcass will be entirely consumed. This decay is caused by animal organisms, in the text called "worm." If the worms do not die, they continue their work, and the body is soon consumed.

When to this picture of utter destruction is added that of fire, we have two destroying agencies,—the "worm" and the "fire,"—which make doubly sure not only that the life will be extinct, but that the carcass will at last be reduced to ashes. The worms, of course, will be unable to destroy the bones of the carcass; Inspiration, therefore, in stressing the idea of total destruction, adds fire to the destroying agencies, so that nothing will remain. The wicked "shall be stubble: and the day that cometh shall burn them up, saith the Lord of hosts, that it shall leave them neither root nor branch." Malachi 4:1. "They shall be ashes under the soles of your feet in the day that I shall do this, saith the Lord of hosts." Verse 3.

We therefore take the texts above noted to amplify the idea of entire destruction. If a fire is not quenched, it will continue burning until the object or objects placed upon it are entirely consumed. The wicked are likened to "the fat of lambs." Psalm 37:20. They are likened to "stubble." Malachi 4:1. They shall burn like "tow." Isaiah 1:31. They shall consume like "thorns." Isaiah 33:12. These substances are all readily inflammable, and if they should be thrown into fire that shall not be quenched it would seem clear that they would be entirely consumed.

The picture presented in the texts we have quoted is that of entire destruction, complete extinction. In Jeremiah 17:27 there is an example given of unquenchable fire. "If ye will not hearken unto Me to hallow the Sabbath day, and not to bear a burden, even entering in at the gates of Jerusalem on the Sabbath day; then will I kindle a fire in the gates thereof, and it shall devour the palaces of Jerusalem, and it shall not be quenched."

It is well known what happened to Jerusalem. In 70 A. D. it was entirely destroyed. As Christ predicted of the temple, there was not one stone left upon another. Matthew 24:2. Fire completed the work of destruction; and the fire was not quenched. If it had been quenched, perhaps part of the city would have been spared; but as it was burned with unquenchable fire, it was completely destroyed.

This is a good illustration of what is meant by "unquenchable fire." It is a fire that is eternal, everlasting, in its results.

There is another example given in the Bible, in Jude 7. "Even as Sodom and Gomorrah, and the cities about them in like manner, giving themselves over to fornication, and going after strange flesh, are set forth for an example, suffering the vengeance of eternal fire."

Sodom and Gomorrah were destroyed by fire. That fire was unquenchable; hence the cities were entirely blotted from the face of the earth. This fire, we are told in the text, is an example of eternal fire. Yet no one would hold that the fire is still burning. It was simply eternal in its consequences, and destroyed the cities entirely.

In like manner, according to the Scriptures, the fires of the last day will entirely consume sin and sinners. They shall be no more. The universe will be cleansed. There will be no more sorrow, sin, or death. Screams of pain and agony of tormented souls will not forever ascend to disturb the peace of eternity. The fire will burn, the worms will do their work, until sin and sinners are completely eradicated. "I have heard from the Lord God of hosts a consumption, even determined upon the whole earth." Isaiah 28:22.

# CHAPTER ELEVEN

# Why Sinners Must Die

IT REMAINS for us to consider a few texts that are sometimes urged against those here presented. Two of these texts are found in the book of Revelation. "The devil that deceived them was cast into the lake of fire and brimstone, where the beast and the false prophet are, and shall be tormented day and night forever and ever." Revelation 20:10. Another is found in Revelation 14:11. "The smoke of their torment ascendeth up forever and ever: and they have no rest day nor night, who worship the beast and his image, and whosoever receiveth the mark of his name."

It is evident that these texts do not speak of mankind in general, but of "the devil," "the beast," "the false prophet," and those that worship them. We will not here go into a detailed exegesis of who these are, but merely notice that the texts quoted refer to a limited number. The texts should, however, be given due weight in any investigation of the subject under consideration.

On the basis of the preceding chapter, no one will have any great difficulty in rightly evaluating these texts in Revelation. We have learned that in dealing with such words as "forever," "eternal," and "everlasting" we must look to their context for their exact meaning. "Forever" does not necessarily mean unending; neither does "eternal" or "everlasting." We do not deny that they often have this meaning, but we wish to emphasize that the context must be the guide in arriving at the exact import of the words. The Greek words from which "forever" and "ever" are taken are defined as follows:

"Greenfield: 'Duration, finite or infinite, unlimited duration, eternity, a period of duration past or future, time, age, lifetime; the world, universe.'

"Schrevelius: 'An age, a long period of time; *indefinite* duration; time, whether *longer* or *shorter.*'

"Liddell and Scott: 'A space or period of time, especially a lifetime, life *ævum;* an age, a generation; *long space* of time, eternity; in plural, *eis tous aiōnas tōn aiōnōn,* unto ages of ages, forever and ever, New Testament, Galatians 1:5.— 3. Later, a space of time clearly defined and marked out, an era, age, period of a dispensation: *ho aiōn houtos,* this present life, this world.'

"Parkhurst: 'Always being. It denotes duration or continuance of time, but with great variety. I. Both in the singular and the plural it signifies eternity, whether past or to come. II. The duration of this world. III. The ages of the world. IV. This present life. V. The world to come. VI. An age, period, or periodical dispensation of divine providence. VII. *Aiōnes* seems, in Hebrew 11:3, to denote the various revolutions and grand occurrences which have happened in this created system, including also the world itself. Compare Hebrews 1:2, and Macknight, on both texts. *Aiōn* in the LXX generally answers to the Hebrew *holam,* which denotes *time hidden* from man, whether indefinite or definite, whether past or future.'

"Robinson: 'Duration, the course or flow of time in various relations as determined by the context; viz., (A) For human life, existence. (B) For time indefinite, a period of the world, the world, in Greek writers, and also in Septuagint and New Testament. (C) For endless duration, perpetuity, eternity. . . . Septuagint mostly for Hebrew *holam,* "hidden time," duration, eternity. Hence, in New Testament, of *long-continued* time, *indefinite* duration, in accordance with Greek usage, but modified as to construction and extent by the example of the LXX, and the Rabbinic views.'

"Schleusner gives as the first meaning of *aiōn,* 'a definite and long-continued time;' i.e., a long-continued but still a definite period of time.

"Wahl has arranged the definitions of *aion* thus: '(1) Time, unlimited duration, *ævum*. (2) The universe, *mundus*. (3) An age, period of the world,' as the Jewish age, Christian age, etc. This reference to Schleusner and Wahl we find in Stuart on 'Future Punishment,' pages 91, 93.

"*Holam,* the Hebrew word which corresponds to the Greek *aiōn,* is applied, according to Gesenius, to things which endure for a *long time,* for an indefinite period. It is applied to the Jewish priesthood, to the Mosaic ordinances, to the possession of the land of Canaan, to the hills and mountains, to the earth, to the time of service to be rendered by a slave, and to some other things of a like nature.

"Cruden, in his Unabridged Concordance, under the word 'eternal,' says:

" 'The words, "eternal, everlasting, and forever," are sometimes taken for a long time, and are not always to be understood strictly. Thus, "Thou shalt be our guide from this time forth even *forever,*" that is, during our *whole life.* And in many other places of Scripture, and in particular when the word "forever" is applied to the Jewish rites and privileges, it commonly signifies no more than during the standing of that commonwealth, until the coming of the Messiah.'

"Dr. Clarke places in our hands a key to the interpretation of the words 'forever' and 'forever and ever,' which is adapted to every instance of their use. According to his rule, they are to be taken to mean as long as a thing, considering the surrounding circumstances, can exist. And he illustrates this in his closing remarks on 2 Kings 5, where, speaking of the curse of the leprosy pronounced upon Gehazi forever, he says:

" 'Some have thought, because of the prophet's curse, "The leprosy of Naaman shall cleave unto thee and thy seed forever," that there are persons still alive who are this man's real descendants, and afflicted with this horrible disease. Mr. Maundrel, when he was in Judea, made diligent inquiry concerning this; but could not ascertain the truth of the supposition. To me, it appears absurd: the denunciation took place in the posterity of Gehazi, till it should become extinct; and under the influence of this disorder, this must *soon* have taken place. The *forever* implies as long as any of his posterity should remain. This is the import of the word, *leôlam*. *It takes in the whole extent or duration of the thing to which it is applied.* The *forever* of Gehazi was till his posterity became extinct.' "—*"Here and Hereafter," Uriah Smith, pages 294-296.*

We doubt that we can do any better than to stress the explanation which Dr. Clarke has given. "This is the import of the word, *leôlam* [forever]. It takes in the whole extent or duration of the thing to which it is applied."

It would therefore seem clear that we must take the words "forever" and "everlasting" in the texts under consideration to be limited in their meaning—"in the whole extent or duration of the thing to which it is applied." If men were immortal, if they were to live forever, if they were incapable of dying, and hence would exist throughout the endless ages to come, then we would interpret the words "forever and ever" to have a like meaning. We have learned, however, that the wicked will not live forever, but eternal life is a gift of God, and is given only to those who value it; we must, therefore, understand the phrase "forever and ever" to cover only the duration of the future existence of the wicked beyond the grave.

We have now examined the leading objections that are raised against the truth set forth in this book. We believe the reader will agree with us that the objections only confirm our position. The Bible does not carry two sets of opinions on any subject. We have abundantly proved from Scripture the future blessedness of the saints. They will be with Christ; they will enjoy with Him life throughout eternal ages. This life is indeed not measured by length only, but, like all real life, by depth. It is not necessarily how long a person lives, but how much he lives that counts; and so, while life for the saints will be unending, eternal life to them will mean more than prolonged existence. It will be the abounding life that Christ came to give. "I am come that they might have life, and that they might have it more abundantly." John 10:10.

The righteous have in this life here on earth shown that they appreciated God's gifts to them, and, as a reward, God gives them life everlasting. With the saints from all the ages, and with the blessed angels in heaven, they will enjoy the companionship and association of those who have lived lives pleasing to God on a sin-cursed earth. They will reap the reward of their faithfulness and devotion to God; forever and ever their songs of praise to God will ascend to Him who lived and died for them, and for whom they have toiled and sacrificed.

The wicked, on the other hand, have not appreciated the Lord. They have not loved Him, nor have they respected the rights of their fellow beings. They have lived for themselves only, and it would be impossible for God to have them members of the community where only love, courtesy, and consideration for the rights of others will exist. They are indeed not responsible for having been brought into the world; but they *are* responsible for the use they have made of the opportunities and responsibilities that came their way. Even though they did not care for life themselves, it was not necessary that they should make life miserable for others by their sin and transgression. They have broken God's commandments, which are the only safe rule of life, and without which no society either on earth or in heaven could exist.

When God makes up His church,—those who shall live with Him forever and ever,—He can admit only those who have shown their willingness to abide by the rules of life— the law of God. If they do not wish to live, God will not force them to live. They have chosen death, and death shall be their portion. Neither in heaven nor on earth shall there exist any hell throughout eternity from which screams and agonizing cries will arise to disturb the peace and purity of the redeemed. God will have a clean universe. Sorrow and sin shall be no more. Though there will be a hell, and though the wicked will be punished for such deeds as they have done in the body, the time will come when both "death and hell" shall be "cast into the lake of fire. This is the second death." Revelation 20:14. When even death and hell are cast into the lake of fire, we may be sure of the eternal extinction of everyone and everything that is opposed to God's rule and righteousness.

Then will come the time foretold by the prophet: "I heard a great voice out of heaven saying, Behold, the tabernacle of God is with men, and He will dwell with them, and they shall be His people, and God Himself shall be with them, and be their God.

"And God shall wipe away all tears from their eyes; and there shall be no more death, neither sorrow, nor crying, neither shall there be any more pain: for the former things are passed away.

"And He that sat upon the throne said, Behold, I make all things new. And He said unto me, Write: for these words are true and faithful." Revelation 21:3-5.

For this time we long. For this time we pray. May it come soon.

## TEACH Services, Inc.
### P U B L I S H I N G

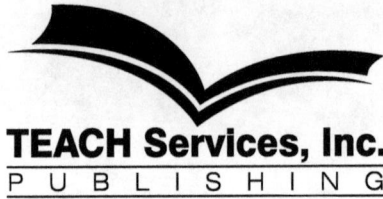

We invite you to view the complete
selection of titles we publish at:
**www.TEACHServices.com**

We encourage you to write us
with your thoughts about this,
or any other book we publish at:
**info@TEACHServices.com**

TEACH Services' titles may be purchased in
bulk quantities for educational, fund-raising,
business, or promotional use.
**bulksales@TEACHServices.com**

Finally, if you are interested in seeing
your own book in print, please contact us at:
**publishing@TEACHServices.com**
We are happy to review your manuscript at no charge.